Got Ghosts???

The Bizarre Tales and Unearthly Adventures of The Ghostbuster Gals

By
Ronnie Rennae Foster
&
Laura Lee Mistycah

LIBRARY OF CONGRESS
CATALOGING-IN-PUBLICATION DATA

Got Ghosts???

The Bizarre Tales and Unearthly Adventures of The Ghostbuster Gals

ISBN: 978-0-9707117-6-2
COPYRIGHT © 2008
LAURA LEE MISTYCAH & RONNIE RENNAE FOSTER

All Rights Reserved
Every part of this book may be used or reproduced in *every* manner with (or without) written permission if the intent is to educate and entertain, ***as long as we get credit for it,*** *especially* in case of brief quotations embodied in critical articles or reviews. Plagiarism however, is a "no - no." If you do not adhere to this dire warning, there may be ghastly ghostly consequences along with some baaaad Karma as well.

Mistyc House Publishing
816 West Francis #244
Spokane WA. 99205
publishing@mistychouse.com

Cover Art and Design by: Laura Bold
Final Lay Out: Russel Davis
Editing by: Sandy Hatfield, Mara Kaunahh, Steve Christilaw, Ruthie Kilpatrick, Vrahc Kohnym
Final Edit: Ronnie Foster and Michele Mitchell

Printing by Ditto's Print & Copy Center
Spokane, WA. USA.

Sharing Our Attitude of Gratitude

There are so many people that have been influential and instrumental in the birthing of this book.

We would like to offer our heartfelt thanks to:

Dannion and Kathryn Brinkley- who have been mentors, friends and an incredible support system for Ronnie, throughout this book as well as her life.

James Van Praagh- who with very little notice came through for us in the eleventh hour, going above and beyond with his endorsement.

Brad and Sherry Steiger- for their support and enthusiasm for our ghost ventures, as well as Laura Lee's other projects, that search for answers while exploring the "unknown."

Laura Bold- who worked tirelessly and patiently through all the changes, to get the front and back cover to what we would consider perfect.

Chandra Caine- who went through personal sacrifice and sleep deprivation to help with formatting the book.

Jack Foster- Ronnie's husband, who exhibited so much patience and understanding, and was very happy to get his wife back once this book went to the printers.

Our clients- who had the faith and courage to hire us.

We would like to especially thank our diligent Editing Staff, who we also consider dear friends:

Sandy Hatfield- who Ronnie could always rely on to be there with the truth and gave her time from her heart.

Michele Mitchell- who has encouraged Ronnie for years in her spiritual growth, and with her usual proficiency offered valuable editing wisdom.

Steve Christilaw- brilliant, professional, and who inspired some exceptional humor in the book.

Mara Kaunahh- for her willingness to edit under short notice and for her unwavering support.

Vrahc Kohnym- for his suggestions that brought new dimensions to this book.

Ruthie Kilpatrick- for her editing insights.

We would also like to thank each other for our ability to work together through any challenges, with ego in check, sharing a sense of respect and grace for our differences.

Foreword

Dear and Courageous Readers,

We chose to write **Got Ghosts??? *The Bizarre Tales and Unearthly Adventures of the Ghostbuster Gals***, in an effort to assist people in transforming their fears and misconceptions into love and understanding, as quickly as possible. The more people that embrace love and compassion as a way of navigating through this reality, the higher the collective consciousness becomes. The more trapped souls that are released and sent "home," the more beneficial it is for the planetary grid system. This release then elevates the Earth's vibration. The higher the vibration, the more evolved humans can become. This is a primary reason that we, Ronnie Rennae Foster a.k.a "Angel Girl" and Laura Lee Mistycah a.k.a "Witchy Woman," have taken on the mantle of Ghostbusters. Ronnie received her nickname, "Angel Girl" because of her connection and resonation with the Angelic Realms. Laura Lee is known as "Witchy Woman," not only because of her physical appearance, but because she practices "Practical Magick."

We do not profess to have all the answers, nor do we think that our way is the only way. Through years and years of research, and by immersing ourselves in the spiritual world, these are the most successful methods and truths we have discovered. Many of these methods were derived from intuitively communicating with our unseen partners, and others from just plain trial and error.

As we evolve as spiritual beings inhabiting physical bodies, our belief systems and truths may also change and evolve as well. One way to decide if the information presented in this book is correct for you is to go into your heart, and see how it feels. If it feels warm and fuzzy, then you can feel safe embracing it. If it makes you sick to your stomach, or sends up "red flags," then discard it. It is not right for you at this time...or maybe any other.

There are a variety of emotions that may be evoked during your passage through our extraordinary world; joy, sorrow, compassion, angst, empathy and forgiveness are just a few. As you move through these stories and begin to realize that there can be an end to suffering, both for the haunted and the hauntee, you may begin to appreciate that there is hope and help available.

Bringing love, light and humor into our work as Ghostbusters, helps us function in this world as well as these strange unearthly realms you are about to explore. We hope you have as much fun reading this book as we did writing it.

Enjoy your journey, and if you learn something that may help you, or someone you know, then we have been successful in our endeavor, and honored our own spiritual contracts as well.

From our hearts to yours,
The Ghostbuster Gals

PS: We tried to elicit the help of ghostwriters for this book, but *they* kept using invisible ink. Oh well...

PPS: All of our stories are true, however, the names may have been changed to protect the haunted.

Table of Contents

1. Who Ya Gonna Call 1
2. What Are Nice Girls Like Us 5
3. In the Beginning 15
4. Demons, & Spirits, & Ghosts ...Oh My! 33
5. Happy House 45
6. Shove-Ins...The Universal Squatters 57
7. Synchronicity...What Are the Odds? 81
8. Ghosts' Stories 97
9. Do You Know Where Your Departed Loved Ones Are? 113
10. Got Ghosts??? So What Do You Do Now? 141
11. Successful Adventures in Ghost Deportation 171
12. In Conclusion 213
13. Who Are The Ghostbuster Gals...Really? 219

Who Ya Gonna Call?

It was a dark and dreary winter night. (So, how did you expect a book about Ghosts to start?) The moon had just begun to creep over the horizon, casting eerie shadows on the sidewalk. In the distance, the scream of an ambulance pierced the air, starting the neighborhood dogs howling.

Kirk approached his front door and stopped, key in hand. He took a deep breath, steeling himself for what he knew lurked inside. *"Oh God, what will it do this time? The attacks are getting worse. Will I be next? I am so uncomfortable in my own home, I am afraid to live here anymore. This was supposed to be the house of my dreams. Now it's turning into my worst nightmare."* As he stood in the doorway, he felt his heart pounding in his chest, his mouth dry with fear. The dread of merely walking in the front door made him feel sick to his stomach.

Kirk was at the point where he just couldn't take it anymore. Thank God, help was on the way! This was the only thing that gave him the courage to walk through that door.

It all began just after Kirk bought this century-old house. It was greatly in need of repair, and he was just the man to do it. Putting his energy into fixing it up was something he looked forward to. However, problems surfaced once he started remodeling. Doors would slam upstairs, and the floors would constantly creak. But that was because the house was so old, right? Kirk tried rationalizing the noises away, but he could not figure out why he was always looking up at the top of the stairs, feeling as if someone was watching him. Someone who made his hair stand on end and creeped him out. It seemed so silly since he knew he was the only one in the house. When his girlfriend stayed over, he wondered if she also felt the dreadful energy that emanated down the staircase. Not wanting to say anything to her because she might think he was crazy, he kept his apprehension to himself.

One evening Kirk and his girlfriend were walking into the living room past the dreaded stairwell, when suddenly a door slammed upstairs. He turned to her and sheepishly asked, "Did you hear that?" When she admitted that she did, he was then brave enough to ask her if she ever felt anything unusual when walking past the stairs. What a relief it was to him when she admitted that she **never** felt comfortable walking past the staircase; in fact, she continued somewhat reluctantly, she didn't feel comfortable upstairs either. Since she was on a roll, she confessed with embarrassment that when he left for work in the morning, she would scurry out of their bedroom and go sleep on the couch downstairs.

Kirk had mixed feelings when he heard her admission. He was happy his bizarre suspicions were confirmed. However, if *it* was also bothering his girlfriend so profoundly, he had to start thinking about what *it* actually was. He could no longer hide in his denial.

Then *it* made *its* presence known so blatantly that there was no doubt this house was truly haunted. One evening while alone in the house, Kirk was upstairs sitting on his bed. The sound of doors slamming broke the quiet, startling him. This time the disturbance was downstairs in the foyer. He took a breath, walked to the stairs, and looked over the railing to double-check the doors he knew he had locked earlier.

A weird, creepy feeling overwhelmed him, as fear consumed Kirk's body and his adrenalin started pumping. "Is anyone there?" he called out with trepidation. At that precise moment as if in answer to his question, he heard a loud crash in the bathroom. Trembling with apprehension, he went to investigate. As he surveyed the site, he was dumbfounded. Bottles of everything that could **not** have possibly fallen off the shelves were lying smashed on the floor. *"No way could they have fallen on the floor by themselves, there was **no way!**"* As the impossibility of this event went through his head, his next thought was... *"I've got to get out of here! I just can't deal with this!"*

From the safety of his mother's house, Kirk thought about his predicament long and hard. He was so used to going to Home Depot for plumbing problems, electrical problems, flooring problems, but he knew that no one at Home Depot would be able to help him fix **this** problem. So, who ya gonna call? That's right. Ronnie received a call from Kirk the next morning.

An appointment was set up for the consultation and ghostbusting. There was way more than "one little ghost" that haunted his property. After three hours of clearing, and sending many trapped souls and entities back where they belonged, Kirk could finally feel comfortable and safe in his own home. (For the rest of this bizarre tale, see the last story in Chapter 11, *Successful Adventures in Ghost Deportation.*)

Got Ghosts???

What Are Nice Girls Like Us... Doing in a Job Like This?

One fateful afternoon, about eight years ago, we were chatting on the telephone. Having worked together for many years on a variety of humanitarian and metaphysical projects, we were reminiscing about all the Weird Sh!t or **W.S.** *(see Chapter 4 for a full definition of this term)* we had been through. It didn't take long to come to the realization that the knowledge and expertise we had gleaned from both our own personal experiences as well as in assisting clients with W.S. was very similar.

At that point we started to joke about how hard it would be to find a *qualified professional* if someone were being haunted or bothered by supernatural things. Laughing, we observed that you just can't find this kind of service under *any* heading in the Yellow Pages. And even if someone did get past all the red tape and slipped an ad in, the prank calls would be endless!

Still chuckling, Laura Lee said, "Hey, with all the experience in W.S. we both have, we ought to go into business together doing Ghostbusting." In unison we howled, "Who ya gonna call???" That subsequently led to the natural answer flying out of Ronnie's mouth, **"GHOSTBUSTER GALS!"** We laughed and hooted, it was just toooo funny. Ronnie actually thought it was a big joke, but Laura Lee was **dead** serious about this new venture and started working toward getting a business plan together.

Even though Ronnie had some experience working with trapped souls, her real impetus to pursue this endeavor was her only sister, Barbara. Barbara developed metastatic breast cancer when she was forty-four years old. Ronnie practically moved into her house to take care of her. When it got very bad, they called in Hospice. It was a pretty rough death, and Ronnie started wondering if her sister had made it across to the Light or if she had gotten stuck between the worlds.

This weighed so heavily on Ronnie's mind that a few months later when she attended a Body-Mind-Spirit Expo, she made sure to catch a panel of experts on the subject. Dannion Brinkley, a man who had already been dead twice by that time, was on the panel. Thinking that he seemed to be the most qualified to answer her question, Ronnie asked him, "Did my sister go into the Light, or is she trapped?" Ronnie was very relieved to hear Dannion say that yes indeed, she had crossed over.

This intrigued Ronnie enough to start thinking about the many souls that might not have been so lucky. What happens to them? It's one of the reasons she became a hospice volunteer with Dannion's organization, The Twilight Brigade/Compassion in Action. Their mission statement is: **No one need die alone.** Ronnie felt that if she could provide a loving presence at the bedside of the dying, maybe that would prevent those souls from getting stuck. Ronnie has since become a Transition Specialist, providing a comfort zone for her to explore those unearthly realms.

Recognizing that there was a great need for helping ghosts cross over, Ronnie thought about Laura Lee's enthusiasm for this new business venture, so she decided to get into the spirit of it. Later that evening, she got a "reality check" on her next Divine undertaking when she started channeling... not her normal fu-fu angelic spiritual messages, but a witty, humorous ghostbusting ad for the newspaper! These words just flowed out onto the page.

> **Are you being bothered by:**
>
> ◆ Pesky Poltergeists?
>
> ◆ Obnoxious Odors?
>
> ◆ Nonsensical Noises?
>
> ◆ Continuous Cold Spots?
>
> **Spirits Getting You Down?**
>
> Who Ya Gonna Call ???
>
> ## Ghostbuster Gals!

Laura Lee thought the ad was great, so just for fun we ran it in an alternative paper. Much to our surprise, we received calls from a local TV news reporter, and from a columnist for the major mainstream newspaper in Spokane. We chuckled in amazement.

Separate lunch meetings were arranged, and that's when it became evident that both these media representatives had one burning question on their minds... Were **The Ghostbuster Gals** for real? After much conversation, questions, answers, and delicious deep fried Oreo cookies, the men all came to the same conclusion...Yes!

We met the TV reporter and his cameraman (Kirk from Chapter 1) the next day for what we thought would be a short interview and tour of a Spokane mansion we had worked on. Apparently, the news crew was so fascinated by the stories they heard, that they actually followed us around for five hours! They also arranged to film us doing a **real live** ghostbusting the next evening at sunset. The reporter confessed to us that the amount of time they were spending was highly unusual for a news story. However, they were so intrigued, the story became top priority and three different segments were aired on the 6:00, 10:00, and 11:00 news! (Kirk later won an Emmy for our story because of his creative camera work, content and editing.)

The newspaper columnist decided to join our group for the ghostbusting expedition. He observed in bewilderment, feeling completely out of his element. (See Chapter 11, Successful Adventures...for the rest of the tale called, *Goodbye Momma*.)

Since that time, we have done several TV and radio shows across the country, a guest appearance on the British TV show, Dead Famous, as well as a follow up on the same local TV news channel. Our stories bring comfort, relief, understanding and humor to those with an open mind and open heart.

~ ~ ~ ~ ~

What We Do

~ Assist trapped and lost spirits in finding their way back to the Light.

~ Open portals or tunnels to the Light to allow spirits to return "home."

~ Close negative or destructive vortexes that can deplete energy or cause illness.

- Remove negative energy beings that have infiltrated someone's personal space.

- Counsel victims of hauntings.

- Help people understand and communicate with disembodied spirits and deceased loved ones that may be trying to give them a message.

- Remove stuck emotions of fear, anger, revenge, guilt, hate and confusion from the Earth's energy grid.

- Clear real estate properties so they sell quicker and so the new owner does not inherit any ghastly ghosts or negative vortexes.

- Clear homes and offices of any negative energy so they feel "cleaner" and lighter.

- Clean up the neighborhood while we are busting a home.

How to Become a Ghost

1. First, you have to die.

2. You have to die in extreme fear, shock, guilt, anger, resentment, hatred, jealousy, ignorance, confusion or in any other dark, heavy, lower vibrations.

3. You have to die with an excessive attachment to people or things i.e.; house, car, money; jewelry, loved one, or pet.

4. The ones you loved hold on to you so tightly, it keeps you earthbound.

5. When the portal "home" opens, you don't see it, you ignore it, or you fear it.

6. You have a misguided sense of duty or a curse that keeps you "landlocked."

7. Not all of these things are required to become a ghost…except number one.

How Not to Become a Ghost

* To get the scoop on how **not** to become a ghost, look for **Got Ghosts??? The Sequel** when it becomes available.

Ghostly Factoids

~ Where do you find ghosts??? (Whisper)… "*They're everywhere…and they are watching you…heh, heh, heh.*" Just kidding! But, you might want to read James Van Praagh's new book, *Ghosts Among Us,* or check out some of Brad Steiger's books on the paranormal to understand just how prevalent ghosts really are.

~ Most ghosts do not realize they are dead and suffer a kind of amnesia or brain fog.

~ Ghosts retain the same personality as they did when they were living.

~ Negative ghosts feed off fear and anxiety. The more afraid you are, the stronger they become.

~ Ghosts do not experience time the same way we do.

~ If ghosts are occupying the same space, they do not necessarily see each other.

~ Even a "good" ghost is bad for our electromagnetic field and can cause weakness, energy depletion and illness in the body.

~ Many people that commit suicide do not cross over and therefore become ghosts. They then experience a time loop and re-live their death along with the events surrounding it over and over and over and over...

It's a Dirty Job, But Someone's Got to Do It

As Ghostbusters, we now have more than eight successful years of professional experience helping people with their unearthly problems, as well as releasing trapped souls from their ghostly plight. We have seen many media shows and read many stories about ghost hunters. What bothers us tremendously is that these "professionals" come in with their sophisticated equipment, and prove that there are ghosts present, but they never seem to care about assisting those ghosts in finding their way "home."

One of Ronnie's favorite shows is *Ghost Whisperer*. The main character is always concerned about helping the ghosts cross over into the Light. Maybe it's because James Van Praagh, one of the foremost mediums on the planet, is the co-executive producer. He is one of the leading experts in the world of ghosts, and it carries over into the program.

From our experience, a soul cannot evolve when it's trapped, and in order for it to be fulfilled, it must return to where it came...back to Source.

Ghostbusting is not an easy job. Throughout the years of our ghostbusting endeavors there have been quite a few times that we were kicked in the butt, so to speak, especially in the beginning. It used to knock us out for at least twenty-four hours. Sometimes we would become exhausted before we even started. Once while doing a remote busting in Manila, the ghosts were so powerful with black magick that they put Laura Lee into an etheric drug induced sleep, right in the middle of the busting!

We have found that in many cases, ghosts can sense something is going on and will try to prevent a clearing from happening. In one situation, we worked on the home of a retired NASA rocket scientist. We completed the consultation, then surveyed the property. The ghost eviction was set up for a later date.

That evening a big huge white blemish appeared in the crook of Ronnie's nose. It did not start small and grow as a normal pimple would. No, it literally just appeared. It looked like a big blister filled with white goo. At the same time unbeknownst to Ronnie, the front half of Laura Lee's nose became burnt, blistered, red and disgusting, like radiation poisoning.

The next day we chatted on the phone and when Ronnie mentioned her "little nose problem," Laura Lee was not sympathetic at all, because hers was a hundred times worse! It was then that we realized we were under simultaneous psychic attack from one of the ghosts in the house we had just visited for the initial consultation. Ronnie got lucky. When she recognized what had caused the unsightly blob on her nose, she was able to "uncreate" it. By the next day, it was one hundred percent gone. (Now, what pimple can clear that fast?)

Laura Lee was not quite as lucky. She had been under severe psychic attack from other sources and her nose took nearly two weeks to stop oozing, scabbing and bleeding, and when you are a Witch it's even worse. These days we take lots of minerals and nutrients before we execute a ghostbusting, and we have learned to protect ourselves a lot better as well.

We now invite you to share in some of our trials and tribulations as you continue your journey through our adventurous venture.

Got Ghosts???

In the Beginning...
Our First Unearthly Encounters

Mistycah's Mini Mansion...Laura Lee's Story

One of my first encounters with blatant, non-physical energies and entities was when I discovered them cohabitating in my **own** home! The story begins in the spring of 1991. My husband had just lost his job, we were facing bankruptcy, our home was being foreclosed, and I was in a desperate search to find another place for my family to live. Finally, an elderly lady at our church said she had a house she could rent to us, but it needed a little repair... That was a **gross** understatement!

We were in a time crunch to find a house big enough for our four children as well as one that would allow dogs. (Our dog "Puppy" had been with us longer than the kids had, and was definitely part of the family!) The elderly lady liked our dog and said Puppy would be welcome to stay without a pet deposit. We decided to drive by to get a feel for the place. What a mess! But there was something that mysteriously called to me, and so, being out of options, we reluctantly took her up on her offer without inspecting the inside.

After dinner, we invited a close friend and her three children to accompany the six of us to check out the place. It was cold and windy, and for some reason the front door key would not work. Undaunted, we gained access through the door to the basement boiler room. It felt as if we were about to descend into a dungeon as we opened the basement door. In the midst of spiders, cobwebs, and who knows what else, the children huddled behind us as we fumbled around the doorway with our hands in search of the light switches. As you might have guessed, as in any respectable haunted house, every pull chain and light switch we tried was ineffective. There were no working lights in the "dungeon" at all! In fact, there were only about four light bulbs in the entire three-level house that worked. It seems the last tenants had left their trash and pilfered the bulbs.

Stumbling through this eerie, dark basement with seven worried kids and three anxious adults was reminiscent of going through some creepy haunted house on Halloween, complete with all the strange noises and weird vibes you get when you don't know what's around the corner...or in this case, even where the next corner was! As we walked past the huge boiler...PRROUUMMM! It turned on, scaring the stuffings out of all of us! On the bright side, it created at least a little light so we could see our way out.

Finally, we made it through the boiler room labyrinth, past the landing, and down the two stairs to a sunken area that was once a grand ballroom. This room took up the entire length of the house and three-quarters of the width. The large windows made it easier to see, as the moonlight filtered through the trees, casting surrealistic shadows into the room.

On the far wall was a great fireplace large enough for an adult to stand in if you ducked your head, but there was so much broken furniture and garbage strewn all over, that it was hard to make our way to it. There was strange graffiti on the walls, and it was evident that many a drug party had gone on in this place.

We turned back to the landing and found a large closet or storeroom between the ballroom door and the stairs. It was so dark you couldn't see inside, but the hair on the back of our necks stood up and we all got the Hee-bee-gee-bee's. We quickly closed the door. (This room was later affectionately called, "The Skeleton Closet.")

In the Beginning...Our First Unearthly Encounters

In a procession, we started our trek up the winding, creaky steps from the basement where more cobwebs met us in the nearly dark stairwell. Reaching the main level, we discovered that there was only one dim bulb that worked on the entire floor, so again moonlight was the major source of illumination. This main floor hosted an entry room, library with a fireplace, living room with a fireplace, kitchen, pantry and laundry room. Between the laundry room and the kitchen was a half-baked excuse for a bathroom. It had never been properly plumbed and was originally a screened in porch. There was definitely some Weird Sh!t in that room!

As we explored, we noticed some of the windows were cracked and broken in different rooms. The sheer curtains were blowing in and out of those windows as the wind whistled eerily through the openings. There were huge gaping holes in the lath and plaster where some pipes had broken. After the pipes were fixed, the plaster had never been replaced. Strange odors loitered in different areas. I was starting to wonder, *"What the #!%* have we gotten ourselves into!"*

Anxiously, we trouped up to the top floor to see what awaited us. One light at the top of the stairwell worked, as did one more in a closet, so either end of the floor was very poorly lit. We found two bathrooms, four bedrooms, (two with summer porches) and one very small room. We were greeted by broken windows, falling plaster, peeling paint, and wooden floors that could give bare feet unsolicited slivers.

As my friend and I were giving the house a *mental make over*, I was psychologically trying to maintain my own composure, all the while in disbelief at the desperate situation that was forcing us to move into this 4,000 square foot "Hell Hole."

In the meantime, my daughter Ma' Lady, who was about four years old then, kept tugging on my skirt and mumbling something. Finally I stopped my conversation and creative visioning of how to redeem the house and said, "What is it...what do you want?" She whispered, "Mommy, I don't want to **die** here!" I laughed and replied, "Ohhhhhh honey, you mean you don't want to **live** here, right?" (Our present house was a very nice place we had custom built. We had been living there for five years, and she and her three brothers were quite fond of it. I'm sure she just couldn't figure out what would possess us to leave that warm fuzzy house and go to this creepy place!) Ma' Lady nodded her head yes in answer to my question...she didn't want to **live** here. (In actuality, I believe her statement was probably a Freudian slip, and she truly thought she might die in this haunted house of horrors!)

Ma' Lady and her brothers didn't understand the adult world of losing employment and the challenges that go along with it, and so we just tried to make the kids think they were embarking on a new adventure...and boy what an adventure that was!

The cleaning and renovation took a long, **long** time, and many bizarre things came to light in the process. For instance, we all felt that there were weird vibes coming from behind the half-baked bathroom door that led to the laundry room. It had a window, and we always had the impression we were being watched from the other side. *Very creepy, especially at night!*

When I did the laundry, **everything** came out wrinkled. Not just a little wrinkled, but like someone had wrung and twisted the clothes, tied them up with string, and then dried them that way. No amount of shaking out the wrinkles before they went into the dryer, fabric softener or dryer sheets, or even ironing would make a difference. Baffled, I spent much time and effort trying to remedy the situation.

Polyester fabrics seemed to wrinkle worse than natural cotton ones, and the static that came out of the clothes dryer was so bad, it would have brought Frankenstein back to life! Such intense sparks and crackling were produced, it made my hair stand on end. The incessant static bothered my eyes so much that I had to shut them and turn my head away as I took the clothes out! Laundry was not my favorite household chore to begin with...now the task had been demoted to torture.

Many other strange things started happening after we moved in. Our kids, who were totally potty trained, began wetting their beds again. Much to my horror, this added to the laundry load tremendously! Nonsensical noises and eerie feelings in various parts of the house were commonplace. The kids were afraid to be alone in certain rooms, and to top it off, the toilet next to the master bedroom would inexplicably flush by itself every night around 10:00. We humorously called it our, "**Potty-geist.**"

After starting to put the pieces together, and concluding that some things were just **not right** in this place, I decided that something had to be done to make this house easier to live in. This was my first personal attempt to remove ghosts, or whatever it was that was causing the strange phenomena occurring all over my house. I gathered all the information I knew from my scripture reading as well as my metaphysical awareness. After getting opinions from both my church friends and my spiritual friends, I began to work on the house.

I first put live plants in areas that needed "life" in them. Painting the rooms white, and laying carpet did a tremendous job brightening up the place, and the energies started to shift. I then meditated relentlessly, putting "psychic lights" in every dark space in the house; in the basement, in the closets, under the stairs, under the beds, behind the boiler, in the icky junk bathroom off the laundry room, and even in the cupboards! Next, I envisioned an imaginary auto reverse tape player with angelic music playing at high volume in each of these places.

Psychically I would check on them periodically, and to my surprise the tape players in the nastiest areas came up missing...they just vanished! Sooooo I just simply replaced them, and resumed my vibration-raising agenda. I did this persistently for several weeks, when I noticed remarkable things starting to happen. The clothes began coming out of the dryer with less wrinkles. I was amazed! I wasn't quite sure if it was just coincidence or if what I was doing really had an effect.

I continued this bombardment of light and music, and everything in the house started settling down. I even got up the intestinal fortitude to clean out the creepy bathroom behind the laundry room, solving a lot of the problems in that area. The static and wrinkles de-creased even more. My plan was working! I continued this regime, adding things here and there as I was inspired to. Within a few more weeks, to my delight, the clothes coming out of the dryer were now *wrinkle free*!

I routinely worked with the energy in the house. The only thing that remained was some sort of frightened entity in "The Skeleton Closet" that conveyed the message, "Please don't make me leave." So I shut the door, sent it some warm fuzzies, and figured it was harmless. This was one of the first experiences I had realizing I could communicate with unearthly energies and entities. I always had an affinity for understanding the realms of the unseen worlds, and now I was experiencing concrete results of my work and interactions with other dimensions.

I think whatever was lurking behind the laundry room, was creating some sort of electromagnetic field that put very intense static on the clothes as they turned in the dryer. On an energetic level, the higher vibrations stopped the friction and static. The energy in that area was then calmed and neutralized resulting in a less torturous laundry experience.

As I reflect back on the situation, I had no idea at that time, how to open portals and call in the Angels to help people through to the "other side," or even that you **could** do that...until I met Angel Girl. I believe what really happened is that I was unknowingly assisted when I deliberately created such high, light vibrations in the house. The ghosts were then able to connect with the Light and go "home."

Ronnie's Realization

I'm Not Crazy!

As I started my journey in this life, I was taught to believe in God. When I began thinking for myself as an early teen, I felt that religion was hypocritical. Not being sure I could trust what I had learned as a child, I became a very pragmatic and practical person, an agnostic that didn't believe in anything I couldn't see. I certainly had no use for astrology, past lives, psychics, UFO's, Angels and all that other mumbo jumbo.

Then one day, in my senior year of college, my life changed. It is amazing what a difference a day makes. My psychology professor, who had his doctorate, called me into his office to discuss my independent study thesis. He suggested I do my research on, now get this...astrology! My jaw dropped as I stared at him incredulously. When I recovered from my shock, I queried, "Are you trying to tell me, that you, a brilliant man, a person with a PhD, actually believes in astrology!!?"

My professor smiled and simply said, "Yes, I do. Very much so." He went on to explain that I didn't have to choose astrology as a research topic if I didn't want to, but he would really like it if I did. Not wanting to disappoint him, (he was kind of cute), I agreed.

At the library, I took out every book I could find on the subject of astrology and began my research. That's when my mind got boggled. The more I read, the more I realized that there was something to this thing I had previously thought of as hogwash. Astounded by the accuracy and precision I discovered, once the whole picture was brought into focus, I became a believer. After this eye opening experience, I started to wonder what else was I wrong about? I had judged out of ignorance and that was a mistake. I began reading books on UFO's and reincarnation with an open mind. I tried very hard to keep my personal opinions to myself concerning things about which I had no knowledge. My consciousness expanded, and so my awakening process was set in motion...slow motion.

I had to move to Boulder, Co. to find God. He wasn't in any of the books I had read. After college, my thirst for knowledge continued. I took a couple of courses at the Boulder "Free School." One was called, *"Sourcery"* (using the word Source as another word for God). I learned what a chakra was, and experienced a new form of energy. It was fascinating. My mind and my soul soaked it up like a sponge. The other class I took was called, *"Alpha Power."* This was where I actually experienced God. Talk about a Rocky Mountain High! That was when my knowingness of the Divine began. I was an agnostic no longer.

My first contact with a spirit that was no longer in a body happened in Phoenix, in 1984. I was totally clueless about this type of phenomenon. At that time, I had decided to take a course at the community college to become a certified Emergency Medical Technician. Now, I had been out of college for at least ten years, and I found myself sitting in a classroom with nurses, pharmacists, scientists as well as other medical professionals. I felt like I was out of my league, but pursued it anyway. I actually went on to be the top student in two classes and won my very own stethoscope! (Not that I'm bragging or anything.)

Our instructor was a paramedic with the Phoenix Fire Dept. and part of our training included an evening of observation, riding with him in the rescue truck. My shift started out uneventful. We went on a couple of routine calls, then went back to the stationhouse to wait and wait and wait. *"Piece of cake,"* I thought. (Of course, I didn't mind being surrounded by all those *hot* fireman, either.) Then, the call came in. **Gun shot to the head!**

In the Beginning...Our First Unearthly Encounters

The ride in the rescue vehicle started my adrenaline flowing as we screamed through red lights, and drove over medians, racing toward oncoming traffic. I was strapped down in the back hanging on for dear life, occasionally getting the courage to peek out the front windshield. I must have looked as white as a ghost! No wonder these guys are so pumped when they reach their destination.

As we arrived on the scene, the fire truck was already there, and a man was lying in the street with an automatic CPR device on his chest. A fireman knelt by his side, manually pumping an air bag that was covering his nose and mouth. There was a look of relief on the faces of all the firemen as our vehicle with the paramedics pulled up.

"Here, start bagging." I was told, as my teacher bent down to get an IV going. I promptly got down on one knee and began squeezing the hard plastic bag every five seconds. After a few minutes, I realized, *this looks a lot easier on TV*. I had to use both hands as my hands are rather small, and it took quite an effort. All sorts of thoughts were running through my mind. *"Am I doing this right? Is this guy going to make it? Is he getting enough oxygen?"*

Finally, the ambulance arrived. They loaded him up and sped off to the hospital. The thrilling task of cleaning up the bloody mess was bestowed upon me. That was enough excitement for one night. Actually, it was enough for one lifetime! Figuring my night was over, I started to calm down a bit. Boy, was I ever wrong! Things were just about to get interesting...very interesting. When we were finished at the scene, we piled into the rescue vehicle and instead of going back to the stationhouse, we followed the ambulance and the fire engine to the hospital.

Arriving at the emergency room, it was pretty easy to track down our patient. As we walked in, there were about five firemen standing as far away from the man on the table as the small room would allow. A doctor was in the process of cutting a triangular incision in his left side to facilitate open heart massage. Apparently, the man was brain dead from the bullet, and they were keeping him alive as an organ donor.

My instructor then grabbed me by the shoulders and maneuvered me into a front row position, right by the doctor just as he is inserting his hand into the man's chest! Good thing I have a strong stomach. Some of the firemen were not so fortunate, as I heard moaning and groaning coming from behind me.

Fascinated, I watched as my instructor impassively pointed out anatomical structures, and examined the wound. A couple of medical students showed up to poke and prod this man who was laying there brain dead, with his body cut open. I was becoming a little annoyed at their insensitivity. They were treating him like a piece of meat. It felt as though they were disrespecting him, and it was making me quite uncomfortable. Now, I had no idea why I was having those type of thoughts, when all of a sudden, something very bizarre happened. I actually felt this man's presence up in the left-hand corner of the room! There was a sense of total confusion and disorientation, as I perceived him looking at his body.

I began to wonder, *"Am I crazy? Is this just my imagination?"* I had heard about things like this, but personally, I had **never** experienced anything like it. However, I just couldn't deny the strong feelings of bewilderment and agitation that were emanating from an area near the ceiling.

Not knowing what to do, and feeling somewhat foolish, I tried mentally talking to the man. I told him it was going to be okay. I felt really weird doing it...but the sensation was so overwhelming. Remember, this was 1984; there weren't too many stories out yet about life after death. I didn't know about "the Light," and at that time, I did not even consider believing in Angels. Can you imagine that! However, for some reason, hearing me communicate with him telepathically seemed to help. He started to calm down. I wish I could say the same for me. It was then time for us to leave.

I thought about that night quite often. *"Was it real? If so, what happened to that man's spirit? What more could I have done?"* Maybe it was part of my awakening process, because I found myself moving away from traditional medicine. Instead of becoming an EMT, I began studying with an Aztec Medicine Man. He was a miraculous healer, able to perform psychic surgery, and had an incredible knowledge of herbs.

It was a 180° turn around for me. I continued to open my mind and heart to the metaphysical world. I must confess there were some aspects of this new "reality" that I had a very hard time accepting. Concepts like, we create our own experiences, we choose our families, as well as there is no such thing as time (past or future), all boggled my mind. But my wise and patient roommate and teacher, Michele, held my hand through it all.

We used to walk around our neighborhood quite often, in Gilbert, Arizona with Michele sharing the knowledge she had already gleaned from the Universe. One day, she turned to me and said affectionately, "You are such a little Light Worker!" I stopped, then faced her quizzically and asked, "What's a Light Worker?" That moment is still so clear to me because I felt something inside ignite, and it started me on the path I am on to this day.

Channeling held a particular interest for me, especially after reading, *Out on a Limb*, by Shirley MacLaine. I actually took a course given by the Tibetan Foundation, on how to become a conscious channel. I hate to admit it, but at the time, I wasn't very good.

I did not have any other contact with disembodied spirits for another ten years. And then, my first authentic ghostbusting occurred, quite by accident.

It was a late November day, 1994. I had been living in Spokane, WA for a few years and just found out that three days prior, a close friend of mine that I hadn't seen in a very long time, passed away suddenly in a car accident. His name was Paul, and he had been a boss, mentor, lover and friend. Believe it or not, we sold encyclopedias...door to door in Boulder, Co. For years, we had what could be considered a roller coaster relationship. I think you get the picture.

Getting ready to go out on some errands, I walked into the bathroom to brush my hair. I still had Paul on my mind, thinking how ironic his death was. Paul was an enthusiastic over-achiever. He pushed his employees unmercifully. The accident that took his life occurred while on a road trip. He had pressed his crew to drive through the night to try to get home for Thanksgiving. While he was napping in the back of the van, the driver fell asleep from exhaustion and hit a guardrail. The impact caused Paul to be thrown out the window, suffering a fatal head injury. This was a man who loved to take risks. He would fly up to Canada to go helicopter skiing, and swim with sharks off the Great Barrier Reefs of Australia. Everything he did, he did with unabashed enthusiasm and a zest for life that was unparalleled. For him to be snuffed out while sleeping was the greatest irony of all.

These thoughts played through my mind as I stood in front of the mirror brushing my hair. All of a sudden, I felt Paul's presence very intensely! I was astounded as I sensed him communicating with me telepathically. The first things he asked were, "How can I be talking to you when you're so far away? Why can't anyone else hear me? What's going on?" To say he seemed extremely confused is an understatement. Lacking any tact at all I simply said, "You're dead!" "I am not!" he retorted. "Yes, you are." I insisted. "You need to go to the Light!"

By that time, there were a few books out about "the Light," although I hadn't read any of them. Paul stubbornly declared, "I am not going anywhere!" It was then that I started to panic. I was at a loss as to what to do. Paul wouldn't even acknowledge that he was dead! My heart pounded as my mind raced for solutions. This was my friend, and he wouldn't go "home" because he thought he was still alive. So, I did the only thing I could think of, which was to call upon the Angels for help. (I had been told by a trance channeler a few years earlier, as well as by other psychics, that I had a strong connection with the Angelic Realm...however at the time, I wasn't sure what that really meant.)

In my mind's eye, I saw three Angels appearing out of what seemed to be a tunnel of white light. "Help!" I implored them. Paul turned around and saw the Angels too. At that instant, he finally realized that what I had been telling him was true. Confusion and anxiety were immediately transformed into resignation and then peace. The Angels surrounded him with love, and he willingly walked off with them through the tunnel.

I was not sure if what I had just experienced really happened. Again I thought, *"Am I crazy? Was this all in my mind?"* I decided not to think about it for a while. Then as luck would have it, I had the privilege of dining with James Van Praagh, world famous psychic and medium who is now the co-executive producer of the TV show *Ghost Whisperer*. I relayed the story to him somewhat sheepishly. However, to my amazement he confirmed the whole event. James told me I wasn't imagining it at all, and I did a great job! Not bad for an amateur. I came to the realization that maybe I wasn't so crazy after all. His encouragement was instrumental in giving me the confidence I needed to do this work.

My next opportunity to connect with ghosts came a couple of years later when my friend, Anya, called and asked if I wanted to accompany her to Glover Mansion while she helped some trapped spirits go to the Light. I had never seen anyone do this type of work before, so I thought I'd tag along. What an eye opener!

Over lunch with Neila, the owner, we were told about the presence of a little girl that was being quite mischievous. She would blow out candles, pull tablecloths off with glasses on them, and actually tug on Neila's clothing to get attention. As Neila sat across from me describing the child's antics, an image started to form in my mind. I could actually feel the girl's spirit and as I opened up to her, she showed me a moving picture of her story. This was the first time I had ever experienced this type of vision.

The child showed me that her parents were the caretakers of the mansion back in the early 1900's. The owner was away in Europe when two thieves broke in. Thinking no one was there, they were surprised by the caretaker and his wife in the foyer. In a state of panic, the thieves pulled their daggers from their belts and proceeded to stab the husband and wife until they were dead. Unbeknownst to them, this poor little girl witnessed the brutal murders of her parents. Neighbors found her the next day in a state of shock.

The amazing thing about this senseless crime was that the two thieves were so rattled after they performed their dirty deed, they fled the mansion without ever taking a thing! In fact, they took off so rapidly, they didn't even close the door behind them. This was fortunate for the child, for that's the reason the neighbors were able to find her. They were concerned when they discovered the door wide open.

The child was then placed in a nearby orphanage still suffering from this hideous trauma and in her weakened condition contracted a lung ailment, dying shortly after. When her soul left her body, she was in such a heavy state of despair that she went to the last place she saw her parents alive, the foyer of the mansion. There she stayed, trying to get the attention of anyone she could. As I related this story to Neila and Anya, both nodded their heads with intuitive agreement.

Moving up to what used to be the child's bedroom, Anya sat in a rocking chair, and we perceived the presence of the little girl with us. Following Anya's lead, we requested that the souls of her parents come back to this dimension to help. I felt a portal of light opening up and saw two benevolent beings, delighted at the prospect of being reunited with their earthly child. When the little girl saw her parents, she ran to embrace them with joyous exuberance. We felt a great reverence and peace as we watched them join together and sensed their gratitude as they disappeared.

We found out later from historical records that the little girl's name was Jolene. Her impish presence was not felt in the mansion again until a few years later while filming a news interview. As I was sharing her story for the camera, Jolene took the opportunity to come back and say, "Thank you."

I followed Anya around the rest of the mansion. Each time we came across an area that had a psychic disturbance, I was able to "see" exactly what was going on and instinctively knew what to do. Anya, (who was an old hand at this), and I worked in sync throughout the releasing of the trapped souls we encountered.

One particularly disturbing incident occurred on the top floor of the mansion. Neila and the rest of the staff would always hear pacing at the top of the stairs. They knew no one was up there because that floor was unoccupied. No one **ever** wanted to go upstairs because it gave them a creepy feeling and was downright scary.

As Anya and I mounted the steps, an overwhelming sense of anxiety and despair descended upon us. The higher up the staircase we went, the more pervasive the apprehension and gloom became. It was then I understood why no one wanted to go up there. I wasn't too sure *I* even wanted to go up there. But on we climbed, and when we got to the top, the atmosphere was so laden with dread it was palpable. It felt like a wall of oppressive misery.

Taking some deep breaths to calm and center myself, I began to perceive telepathic communication with a young, very distraught woman. She was pacing back and forth, in obvious distress. I then began "seeing" the pictures of her life...and death. (Years later, I found out from Anya that her name was Maita.) She had been a maid in the mansion and was subjected to sexual abuse by the tyrannical "lord of the manor." She was a thin, frail young thing and desperate for work. Ireland was her home, and she had no friends or relatives in this country.

One day Maita discovered she was pregnant. It frightened her so because she thought she'd be thrown out in the street, and she wouldn't be able to take care of herself, let alone a baby. Keeping her pregnancy a secret, she wore a large apron to cover her growing belly. Maita never really looked pregnant, because of her emotional stress. She suffered from malnutrition as well, since she didn't have much of an appetite.

When it was time to give birth, Maita went up to the top floor, which was the maid's quarters, and paced and paced throughout her labor. It was very late at night, and no one was awake. When she was ready to give birth, she went into the large claw footed bathtub that was nearby. I saw the baby come out into the water and Maita, out of desperation, allowed her baby boy to drown. Wrapping the child in a white towel, she went downstairs behind the mansion and threw him out with the trash.

Maita's guilt was so overwhelming that not long after she killed her baby, she went upstairs late one night and instead of going to bed, she began pacing, just as she had done when she was in labor. Back and forth she walked, in pain and emotional turmoil, burdened by her tremendous guilt.

Finally, it was time to go into the bathtub. Using the same sharp razor she had used to cut her baby's umbilical cord, she very calmly proceeded to slit both her wrists. I could see the bathwater turn blood red as it oozed from her dying body. (Even as I write this, my heart is pounding, as I am re-living this moment with her and still tapping into her pain and grief.)

While I narrated Maita's story, Anya was right there with me, picking up the same intuitive impressions. There was so much fear and despair it actually left a psychic imprint.

When Maita left her physical body, her guilt, and anguish were so devastatingly heavy that she never even saw the tunnel "home." She proceeded to create a hell for herself, doomed to repeat the events of her labor, giving birth, throwing the baby out, and finally killing herself, over and over again. It was as though she was caught in a time loop. Hence, the pacing that was heard by everyone.

I talked to Maita and told her it was time for her to go back to God. She refused, explaining to me how she didn't deserve to go to Heaven because she didn't give her baby a proper burial. I found it interesting that the major source of her guilt was not that she had killed her newborn, but that she didn't bury him properly, according to the tenets of her religion. I then had to pull a "Monica" from the TV show *Touched by an Angel*. At the time, it was the only thing I could think of to do. So I told Maita, "God loves you. He does not judge you. It's alright to go home now."

All of a sudden Maita's demeanor changed, as this truth began to sink in. Her incessant nightmare was about to end. She breathed a big sigh of relief as she prepared herself to go through the tunnel that was now opened by the Angels. When she finally left, we were in awe of the process that had just occurred, and so very grateful we were able to rescue this woman from her self-generated hell. Oh, and as for the pacing...it was never heard again!

I have Anya and the Glover Ghosts to thank for helping me realize I had a gift for hearing trapped souls and the intuition to know how to help them. My first two experiences were chalked up to coincidence. The third time was the charm.

My services were requested at the mansion again, years later. There was a need for a more extensive clearing.

This time I was prepared. I had my ghostbusting partner Laura Lee with me, and as you shall see in Chapter 11, what a ghastly, ghostly tale that was.

Demons and Spirits and Ghosts... Oh My!

What Does It All Mean?

To offer some clarity on terminology, and to help you navigate your way through our bizarre tales, we are going to go to old Webster to give us various mainstream definitions, followed by some of *our own explanations and insights* into this "unearthly realm."

<u>Archangel</u>: A chief angel or an order of angels

* Some of the Archangels we work with are: Michael, Gabriel, Ariel, and Raphael.

<u>Angel</u>: Literally, messenger: A spiritual being superior to man in power and intelligence; *especially* one in the lowest rank in the celestial hierarchy. An attendant spirit or guardian; harbinger

* Ronnie works very closely with the Angelic Realm. She was astounded when she discovered that Angels do not feel they are superior to humans. They are here in loving support and think of us as heroes because we have chosen to experience this heavy density. At any one time there are many Angels prepared to come to our aid. It is considered an honor. They can help a

synchronistic event take place; help us avoid an accident; whisper encouraging or insightful thoughts in our ear; comfort us when we need it the most. There is no end to the assistance we get from our Angelic friends. It is said that Angels are in service to God. When Angels serve us, they are in essence serving God. There is no difference. One morning in a meditation, the Angels imparted these words of wisdom to Ronnie, "Humanity is the Soul of God."

Apparition: An unusual or unexpected sight; phenomenon; a ghostly figure

* *Aulmauracite: The stone of truth and justice. A beautiful, majestic, black sparkly rock, which is not from this planet. We don't leave home without it, especially when we are ghostbusting! The dust it sheds is called Aurauralite and is just as powerful. (See Chapter 10 for more information on Aulmauracite.)*

Aura: A subtle sensory stimulus; a luminous radiation; an energy field that is held to emanate from a living being

* *Sometimes other people's energy, as well as "unearthly" energy, can get inside your auric field and drain you. It is important to cleanse your aura every now and then. (See Chapter 10 for details)*

Chakra: Any of several points of physical or spiritual energy in the human body according to yoga philosophy

* *Laura Lee believes that chakras are an unnatural, imposed system, deliberately designed for outsiders to gain easy access to our energy. See her article "The Secret Behind the Chakras" at: www.firstwaveindigos.com for more information.*

Clairaudience: The power or faculty of **hearing** something not present to the ear but regarded as having objective reality

Clairvoyance: The power or faculty of **seeing** objects not present to the senses

Clairsentience: The power or faculty to **feel** matters beyond the range of ordinary perception

*****Crystal Child:*** *Highly sensitive, psychic and can be telepathic; came in around the year 2000; veils are very thin.*

Déjà vu: The illusion of remembering scenes and events when experienced for the first time; a feeling that one has seen or heard something before

Demon: An evil spirit; a source or agent of evil, harm, distress, or ruin

* In all of our ghostbusting experiences, we have not come across one demon. We have had clients that thought demons were present, but we have always found it to be a trapped spirit who enjoyed being a bully because his earthly life was so wretched. His ghostly purpose was to create frightening experiences so he could then feed on the fear to make himself stronger.

Now, Ronnie has come across some pretty nasty, ugly fourth-dimensional astral beings that will sometimes come to her before sleep. They look like something out of a B-rated horror movie. The more hideous they would appear, the more Ronnie would laugh and send them love. Then, they would just disappear. They were hoping for a reaction of fear and terror so they could feed off of it. Ronnie put them on a starvation diet!

Laura Lee has had personal encounters with entities and energies that were conjured, digitally created, or came into this universe through the rips in time and space. Some of these entities defy all logic and need to be dealt with on a case-by-case basis. In this respect, one might consider these entities "demons" because of their demeanor and intent, but she does NOT believe in the "church" perception of demons as minions that do the Devil's bidding.

Devil: The personal supreme spirit of evil often represented in Jewish and Christian belief as the tempter of mankind, the leader of all apostate angels, and the ruler of hell

* The Ghostbuster Gals do not believe in the Devil. The Devil is a fabrication of man in an effort to control for the sake of power.

Dowse: To use a divining rod: to find (as water) by dowsing

* Laura Lee uses muscle response testing to dowse information during ghostbusting. She has been dowsing this way for over eighteen years and has become very proficient. With her expertise and knowledge using this method, her accuracy rate is ninety-four to one hundred percent. She also uses an Aurauralite pendant as a dowsing tool.

Fairy: A mythical being of folklore and romance usually having diminutive human form and magic powers

* <u>First Wave Indigo</u>: First Wave Indigos are beings who walked into bodies on this planet between 1969 and 1987, (with about thirty percent arriving in the 50's and stragglers on both ends of the timetable). They are highly intelligent, highly psychic, and highly empathic and here on a service mission. These people have been misinterpreted and many have been labeled slow, dyslexic,

uncooperative and rebellious. Our school systems were not able to identify and chart their aptitudes because many of them have information that is difficult to define. In addition, they process information intuitively and internally so they cannot show how their answers were derived. This caused many of them to be unjustly accused of cheating. For more information go to: www.firstwaveindigos.com.

Ghost: A disembodied soul; *especially*: The soul of a dead person believed to be an inhabitant of the unseen world or to appear to the living in bodily likeness

God: The supreme or ultimate reality: As the Being perfect in power, wisdom, and goodness who is worshiped as creator and ruler of the universe: *Christian Science*: The incorporeal divine Principle ruling over all as eternal Spirit: Infinite Mind

* Connectedness with God/Goddess energy is our ultimate way of approaching life, which carries over to our work. It's the only way to fly.

Guardian Angel: An angel believed to have special care of a particular individual; *broadly*: Savior, protector

* Each and every soul on this planet has a Guardian Angel with them from the moment they are born until they make their transition "home."

Haunt: To visit or inhabit as a ghost: To appear habitually as a ghost

Hell: A nether world in which the dead continue to exist; the nether realm of the devil and the demons in which the damned suffer everlasting punishment: A place or state of misery, torment, or wickedness

The word that Jesus almost always used for "hell," is NOT a direct reference to an otherworldly place of eternal torment and damnation. Instead, it was the name of the place where garbage was dumped and burned outside the Southwestern gate of Jerusalem known as Gehenna.

The Ghostbuster Gals do not believe anyone is ever cast into Hell by God. Souls, because of their guilt, fear, ignorance, or lack of self-esteem may choose or create a hellish existence after death, but it is their own thoughts that manifest their own "Hell."

God is all about Love and does not judge. The judgment occurs during the life review process all souls eventually go through. They get to experience the direct results of their interactions with everyone they have ever encountered...the good, the bad and the ugly. Then THEY are the ones that judge their own life. Read **Saved by the Light** *by Dannion Brinkley for more information about the life review process.*

Incubus: An evil spirit that lies on persons in their sleep, *especially*: One that has sexual intercourse with women while they are sleeping - In medieval Europe, union with an incubus was supposed by some to result in the birth of witches, demons, and deformed human offspring. The legendary magician Merlin was said to have been fathered by an incubus

* Ronnie has had an encounter with an incubus that would certainly contradict old Webster. While living in Phoenix she was visited by a being that for all intents and purposes looked like a demonic animal. He had pointed ears, a hairy face, a black nose, but kind and gentle eyes. For some reason she was not afraid of this being. She saw deeper than the physical nature of this creature. They proceeded to make love, in a

peaceful and tender manner. And then he was gone. The next day she told her roommate, Michele, about the strange event that occurred during the night, and much to her astonishment, Michele admitted the creature had visited her two nights before! Ronnie thought she might have just been dreaming even though it felt so real, but when Michele described the being in detail, she knew it really happened.

Years later, Ronnie was having a discussion with a bestselling author friend of hers and he told her of an event that happened to him with a creature that was startlingly similar to hers. He also perceived this being to be kind, gentle and benevolent.

Karma: *Often capitalized:* the doctrine of fate as the inflexible result of cause and effect; the theory of inevitable consequence.

* Laura Lee believes that another aspect which needs to be considered is that Karma could be interpreted as Hell, both here and in the Hereafter. When people have accumulated "bad Karma" and it comes back to haunt them, it can certainly can feel like Hell. Read Laura Lee's article on Lady Karma to find out how she was imprisoned, causing many unjust outcomes and how she was recently set free.
www.firstwaveindigos.com/pages/karma.html

* Kryahgenetics Egg: This is a tool that we use in our Ghostbustings. It was "brought" through to this dimension by Laura Lee. Some very complex and powerful, ancient encoded healing symbols are implanted in this Egg. (See Chapter 10 for a picture, and instructions.)

Ley Line: The electromagnetic pathway between two energetic power points, such as the pyramids, Stonehenge, ancient temples and other spiritual centers. Ley Lines can be compared to the meridian lines between acupuncture points of the Earth.

Lucifer: A fallen rebel archangel, the Devil, from Old English, from Latin, the morning star, from *lucifer* light-bearing, from *luc-, lux* light + *-fer* -ferous -- more at light: Used as a name of the devil

* Does it make any sense to you, that a being whose name literally means "light-bearing" could be so feared, loathed, and hated? This to us is the ultimate "Oxy Moron." Perhaps we have had a major misperception, and we have feared something that is not actually frightening at all. It is astounding how corrupted the truth has become. Lucifer is very much the opposite of how many have perceived him. Some believe that Lucifer made the ultimate sacrifice when he volunteered to take on the mantle of darkness, so we could know the Light.

Medium: Go between, intermediary; an individual held to be a channel of communication between the earthly world and a world of spirits

* Ronnie's diminutive stature makes her, "A Small Medium at Large," and Laura Lee is most certainly a "Happy Medium."

Metaphysics: Of or relating to the transcendent or to a reality beyond what is perceptible to the senses; supernatural

New Age: Of, relating to, or being a late 20th century social movement drawing on ancient concepts especially from Eastern and American Indian traditions and incorporating such themes as holism, concern for nature, spirituality, and metaphysics: Of, relating to, or being a soft soothing form of instrumental music often used to promote relaxation

Psychometry: Divination of facts concerning an object or its owner through contact with or proximity to the object

Poltergeist: A noisy usually mischievous ghost held to be responsible for unexplained noises (as rappings)

* We have found that most poltergeist activity can be attributed to the presence of an Indigo that is having an emotional outburst or inner turmoil.

Portal: Door, entrance, *especially*: a grand or imposing one: The approach or entrance to a bridge or tunnel

Precognition: To know beforehand - clairvoyance relating to an event or state not yet experienced

Satan: *noun*: Middle English, from Old English, from Late Latin, from Greek, from Hebrew *sAtAn* adversary: The adversary of God and lord of evil in Judaism and Christianity

* The Aramaic word satan literally means accuser. It has also been interpreted as the ego, which can tend to stand in judgment of things outside itself. It is what holds the illusion of separation from God. Ego stands for Edging God Out.

We believe it is the unbalanced egos of tyrannical bullies that have created the evil in this world. It seems that society has a propensity towards using scapegoats for their own shortcomings, so they needed something to point the finger at, and Satan (The Devil) got the rap.

Spirits: A supernatural being or essence; **soul**: An often malevolent being that is bodiless but can become visible; *specifically*: **ghost**: A malevolent being that enters and possesses a human being: The immaterial intelligent or sentient part of a person

Succubus: A demon assuming female form to have sexual intercourse with men in their sleep

Synchronicity: The coincidental occurrence of events and especially psychic events (as similar thoughts in widely separated persons or a mental image of an unexpected event before it happens) that seem related but are not explained by conventional mechanisms of causality; used especially in the psychology of C. G. Jung. (See Chapter 7 for some amazing Synchronicities.)

Telekinesis: The production of motion in objects (as by a spiritualistic medium) without contact or other physical means

Telepathy: Communication from one mind to another by extrasensory means

Visions: Something seen in a dream, trance, or ecstasy: A supernatural appearance that conveys a revelation: A manifestation to the senses of something immaterial: Direct mystical awareness of the supernatural usually in visible form

Vortex: A region within a body of fluid in which the fluid elements have an angular velocity; something that resembles a whirlpool

* An energy field that can have either a positive or negative polarity and attract the same type of energy to it.

Witch: One that is credited with usually malignant supernatural powers; a woman practicing usually black witchcraft often with the aid of a devil or familiar: An ugly old woman: A charming or alluring girl or woman: A practitioner of Wicca

* *It is interesting that Webster gives the most accurate definition last and the least accurate first. In fact, the entire sequence seems to be backwards. Here is a list of what Real Witches practicing Wicca ARE about. (Taken partially from Silver Raven Wolf's book, "Teen Witch.")*

Real Witches do not hurt people physically, mentally, spiritually or magically.

Real Witches do not work black magic or kill animals for rituals.

Real Witches do not call themselves "Warlocks" which means "Truth Twister."

Real Witches do not eat babies or drink the blood of animals, summon Demons, or worship the Christian Devil and use satanic symbols.

Real Witches believe in a God/Goddess - Lord/Lady Creator of the Universe.

Real Witches believe in Karma, what you give out comes back times three, therefore avoid doing hurtful things.

Real Witches honor all positive religious/spiritual paths and respect the Earth and all her inhabitants.

Real Witches use spells and magic to heal themselves and others.

Wicca is a spiritual path of enlightenment, with a motto of "Harm None"...and that is just the beginning.

Weird: Of, relating to, or caused by witchcraft or the supernatural: magical; of strange or extraordinary character: Mysteriously strange or fantastic: May imply an unearthly or supernatural strangeness or it may stress queerness or oddness

* *<u>W.S.</u>: Acronym for Weird Sh!t: Unexplainable phenomena; experiences or events that defy logic; things that are highly irregular or coincidental.*

Laura Lee's siblings for the most part, have no interest in any of her expertise or professional skills, and call what she does, "Weird Sh!t." As time has progressed and some of her work and research have come to their attention, they have put some labels on what they perceive she's into...and being good Mormons, have used acronyms to describe these conditions.

W.S. = Weird Sh!t
R.W.S. = Really Weird Sh!t
R.R.W.S. = Really, Really Weird Sh!t
R.W.S.S. = Really Weird Scary Sh!t

We think you can tell by the description and order placement, that there are degrees and intensities of W.S. Recently Ronnie has added a new category, and it is one of our favorites.

F.W.S. = Funky Weird Sh!t

We have left some space on this page, just in case you want to add some of your own versions of W.S.

Happy House

There once was a little boy named Joshua who was born in the house where his parents lived. This house was very unhappy because it was cursed. In fact, his mother, Allison, had already experienced three miscarriages. How very sad.

When Joshua arrived in this world, there was much celebration, but then twenty minutes after his birth, he turned blue and was rushed to the hospital. He spent the next seven days in ICU. His mother was told there was a ninety percent chance her little boy would die, but Allison knew in her heart, that he would make it. The doctors couldn't give her any explanation as to why her son had such severe respiratory problems and needed six medications plus steroids just to breathe.

Finally, Allison was able to bring her infant son home. Many times as she sat with him during the night, she couldn't help wondering if perhaps the breath he was breathing might be his last.

Joshua had to have breathing treatments at the hospital for the next ten years. No one was aware of the curse. They only knew that many people in the neighborhood seemed to have had more than their share of physical ailments.

Strenuous activities had to be greatly curtailed for Joshua because of his chronic condition, so he spent a lot of time alone, inside the unhappy house, playing with his "imaginary" friend Tommy, who was four years old. Joshua, who was also four at the time he discovered his friend, continued to have conversations with Tommy and play with him as if he were real. His mother didn't think much about it as she felt it was common for children to have "imaginary" friends.

Throughout the years, many abnormal and sometimes frightening phenomena occurred inside this cursed house, especially in the basement. Then things started escalating to the point that Allison decided she needed to do something about it for the sake of her family and her sanity. A Catholic priest was brought in to bless the four corners of the house. Allison was then given holy water to spray if there were any more disturbances.

The priest's purification seemed to ameliorate the symptoms for a short time, and things did settle down a bit, but it didn't take long for distressing things to start happening again. This time it was even worse!

What's a mother to do?

Allison shared her dilemma with a friend of hers who fortunately happened to be a client of Ronnie's. However, it took another few weeks for her to get up the courage to contact us. We set up a consultation getting the history of the house and information on the strange and bizarre events that had transpired.

Here is a partial list of the W.S. that was going on in this very unhappy house.

- ~ Joshua told us that when he was four, he had seen a "bluish white kid" his age in the kitchen. He called the boy Tommy, who told him, "I'm lost." Joshua would open the basement door because he knew Tommy was afraid and wanted it open. Sometimes the door would open by itself.

- ~ Allison said there was an obnoxious odor in Joshua's room, and he was afraid of something in his closet.

- ~ When they were all in the basement, they could hear someone walking around upstairs.

- ~ In the kitchen, there was an inexplicable cold spot under the cabinet where the old sink had been removed. It was so cold, they actually used it as a refrigerator, even in the summer!

- ~ They could hear someone shuffling papers in the basement, when all members of the household were accounted for.

- ~ When going up the basement stairs, they felt as if someone was going to grab their feet.

- ~ There were stains on the basement walls that they could not cover up, no matter how many times they painted.

- ~ Electrical disturbances occurred throughout the house, and they heard someone or something knocking on the wall.

- ~ The snails in the aquarium in the basement multiplied at an alarming rate.

- ~ Allison saw a white light with blue hovering over her son when he was an infant. We discovered that this light was her brother who had passed. He was protecting Joshua as he lay in his crib.

It was no surprise that we not only discovered ghosts but a very malicious curse as well. Another appointment was set up to do the clearing.

On "Busting Day," we pulled up to the house and immediately felt a sense of foreboding. The nice middle class neighborhood seemed heavy and oppressive. We had heard that there was a lot of ill health in the vicinity, and now we understood why. Turning to each other we commented about how this house, did **not** look happy. It literally appeared to be frowning and downright miserable!

Allison welcomed us at the front door and breathed a sigh of relief as she escorted us into her dining room. We gave the house a once-over and then set up our altars. Witchy Woman placed her Dragon/Aulmauracite altar in the basement, and Angel Girl set up her angelic altar and crystals in Joshua's room.

While in meditation, Ronnie found out why Joshua was so afraid of the closet. The energy emanating from it was very negative and disturbing. Knowing there must be some W.S. going on, she decided to wait for her partner, the Queen of W.S. to tackle it.

As Ronnie went deeper into her meditation and prayer, she was able to connect with the little boy, Tommy. This is the story she received telepathically.

When Tommy Strickland was about three-and-a-half, his mother had become ill and died. His father, Andrew, was not able to handle the loss and started drinking heavily. A few months later, he lost his job. Poor Tommy always seemed to be in the way. He reminded his father of the wife he lost...same color hair and eyes. Andrew had no patience for his young son, so whenever Tommy would try to get his attention (which was quite often), he would get locked in the basement. It terrified Tommy when that basement door would close and he would be left alone in the dark.

One late afternoon, Tommy was feeling very sad and lonely, missing his mother so very much. When he started to cry, Andrew got angry and told him to get in the basement. Tommy resisted, crying louder. Andrew grabbed him by the arm and walked him down the first few steps. As he let go, Tommy tried to grab on to him, begging and pleading not to be locked in the dark basement. Irritated and annoyed, Andrew jerked his arm away and Tommy went tumbling down the stairs. His little head hit the concrete floor, and he lay there semi-conscious. It took several hours for him to die, alone, confused and afraid. His father, wrapped up in his own self absorbed, drunken misery, ignored him.

Authors Note: *Many of the stories for this book were written years after the actual ghostbusting took place. Sometimes our notes are a little thin and our memories even thinner since we are in an altered state when the information is received. However, there seems to be a psychic link that continues to connect us with the ghosts we rescue.*

That connection helped us with many of the details needed for this book. However, there was some confusion for us as to what Andrew did with Tommy's body. We just could not get any clarity about it, and it bothered us. Then Ronnie realized her link was with Tommy, and his vision ended when he passed, so we couldn't know what became of his physical form.

Andrew felt very guilty for causing the death of his son. He would sit at his work table in the basement for long periods of time, sifting over the paperwork of his mounting debt...drinking and getting more and more depressed. He finally got to the end of his rope metaphorically, then literally. The End.

Andrew's spirit remained trapped in the basement full of anger, guilt, and despair.

Turning her attention to the cold spot under the cabinet where the old sink used to be, Ronnie began to get nauseous. As the visions started to come, she got sicker and sicker. She could see a man dismembering a woman in the sink with a hatchet. Blood splattered everywhere; pieces of bone and chunks of flesh covered the counter. It was absolutely grotesque!

While trying to bring up the information for this book, Ronnie could vividly see the mutilation and feel the queasiness in her stomach again, but she had to call Laura

Lee because she couldn't remember anything about the poor woman that had been hacked to pieces. Finally, she had the insight that she was not tuning into the actual ghost, but the energy that had been projected in that area. That's why there were no details forthcoming at the time. The ghost was not there for some reason, only the intense, brutal, cold, residual energy, emanating from the psychopath when he violently murdered this woman. That energy was stuck on a continual loop.

Meanwhile down in the basement, Laura Lee was picking up on some funky energy which she felt was responsible for causing the over abundance of snails in the aquarium. For some strange reason, before leaving to meet Ronnie, she was gathering up her ghostbusting paraphernalia, and picked up a conch shell that was on her altar. She received a psychic hit that she would need it, even though this made no sense to her at all. However, she took it anyway.

As Laura Lee was putting up her altar, she unloaded the shell and thought, *"Hmmmmm...I bet I can use this shell as an energy signature to put the out-of-control snail population back into balance."* She was sure glad she followed her gut feeling! After setting up the altar, complete with lit candles and incense, she took the conch shell in her right hand and the Aulmauracite stone of truth in her left hand, and then swirled them in a circular manner while doing something in her head that is hard to explain. Then, with intense mental and psychic focus, she projected total balance/homeostasis into the aquarium. Taking a deep breath, she locked this energy in place.

Now, for the creepy energies in the hall where the water heater closet was located. Laura Lee first smudged the heck out of the area. Then using similar psychic focus as with the conch shell, she rubbed two Aulmauracite rocks together to scrape "magic dust" off them onto the water heater, the entire closet and the hallway where the energy was the strongest. Her intent was to clean the debris out and clear the magnetic glitches that were attracting and then trapping funky, disturbing energies in this area. It took a couple of minutes for the dark, heaviness to start lifting. Soon it was completely gone!

The next item was the wall that had the paint resistant stains. Laura Lee tapped the wall where the stains were, and once again used her psychic abilities to clear the cause of the discoloration, whatever that might be. There seemed to be some resistance at first and then poof, it cleared. Now the entire basement felt lighter and free of the foreboding, frightening energies that had been lurking there for decades. All that was left in the basement now were the ghosts, and that was a job she would collaborate on with Ronnie.

We rejoined each other in the kitchen to share the information we had received. After hearing what Laura Lee had encountered in the basement, Ronnie now understood what was creating the disturbance in Joshua's closet. Sitting right above the water heater, the negative energy vortex Laura Lee discovered had traveled up through the floor and invaded the closet as well. As a team, we went back in the closet, dismantled the vortex, and cleaned up the energy.

The next step was to help release Tommy and Andrew from their "living" hell. A portal was opened, and the Angels were there immediately to take Tommy home. Andrew was another story. He was in such a deep funk, that he could not recognize the Light.

Putting our heads together, we decided to ask Andrew's wife to assist in the rescue. Merribelle, full of grace and forgiveness stood at the entrance of the portal with her hand outstretched to Andrew. The vibration of the woman he loved, woke him up to his surroundings. As his eyes beheld his beautiful wife, he ran to her in tears. Weeping uncontrollably, he sobbed, "I'm sorry, I am so, so, sorry...Tommy..." He was so filled with grief and shame that he couldn't finish speaking. Merribelle quietly took his hand and started up the portal, murmuring words of consolation.

Remaining in the kitchen, Laura Lee then released and transmuted the reverberating, dark, despicably brutal, energy under the cabinet where the old sink used to be. However, as Ronnie tuned into this negative force, she started to connect with an energy that was located outside the home, behind the garage.

She intuitively felt that it might actually be the ghost of the young woman that was hacked to pieces. The psychopath must have murdered her outside, and then brought her body in the house to do his dirty work.

We were now ready to take on the backyard, knowing that there was a great deal of Native American energy present. After our meditation and joint collaboration, we discovered a "white man's curse" upon the land in this particular neighborhood.

Ronnie set up a new altar in the yard with her sacred Native American ghostbusting paraphernalia. When Ronnie tried to light the sage in her smudge bowl, her "fire stick" (a Bic lighter) acted like there was no fuel. She clicked and clicked and it just would not light. Laura Lee had to go back to her altar and find some matches to finally get the sage lit. (It is interesting to note that Ronnie's lighter worked perfectly when she got home!)

After the candles were lit, and the area was smudged, Ronnie tuned into a very strong and stately spirit. His name was Chief Standing Elk, and this is what he told her. "The white man is a plague upon our nation. They deserve to have the breath sucked out of them!"

Since the white man came, raped the earth, and slaughtered the innocent natives, the Chief had put a curse upon them. That curse remained potent for years, and was still making the men in the area sick, each in a different way. This curse didn't appear to bother the females, just the white men. Interestingly enough, this curse did not affect Allison's husband since he was of Mexican descent and not considered a "white man."

After communicating with the Chief and sensing the pain and destruction the white man had caused his people, it was not too hard to understand why he would feel so hostile. Making a great sacrifice, the Chief and two of his strongest braves had to stay in the spirit world to sustain the curse and keep it alive.

Ronnie put on her medicine necklace, and her Chanupa (sacred pipe) was placed on the altar. Standing Elk could not quite fathom how this was possible since he had not seen a female pipe carrier before. However, he recognized that she must be "honorable" and someone with a strong spirit in order for her to carry one.

As we began to open a portal to the Light, Ronnie turned to Laura Lee and questioned in amazement, "Did you see that?" Laura Lee replied, "It looks like a teepee!" Ronnie was tickled that they saw the same thing at the same time (which actually happens frequently). This was the first time we had experienced a portal in the shape of a teepee. But it made sense, since it would help the natives relate to it.

White Buffalo Calf Woman, who first brought the pipe to the Indians, came through the teepee to escort the Chief and his braves home. We kept the portal opened and attracted the attention of many other natives that had been trapped in the area.

We make it a standard practice to clear the neighborhood with each ghostbusting. Knowing there were other ghosts and animal spirits in the vicinity that needed to be released, we decided to open up another portal. It was important to make sure that the woman Ronnie discovered behind the garage would be included in this spirit rescue.

As we began to establish another portal once again we both saw the same vision at the same time. It was some kind of portable, accordion looking thing that expanded to full length and then opened! We just looked at each other in amazement, as this was also a new experience for us. It seemed to be a "portable portal" or what we now endearingly call, "A Porta-Portie." (We have since found a cousin to this, that we nicknamed a "Potty Porta-Portie" for the Weird Sh!t to go in.)

Surveying the area, we were satisfied that the curse had been nullified, and the house could be certified ghost free. We were exhausted as we packed up to leave. Just before we got into the car we both turned back to take one last look, and we were gratified to see that the house actually looked happy! The difference was so tangible, we knew our work was done.

Here are some excerpts from emails Allison sent us over the next few weeks:

> *"Overall, Joshua feels safe and happy."*
>
> *"There is so much peace and love in this house."*
>
> *"Things are going great around here. Joshua has a touch of the flu and a cold. The miracle is that he has not had one asthma attack with it. That is amazing! As a matter of fact he has not had an asthma attack since the Wednesday that you did the ghostbusting!"*
>
> *"I keep forgetting to tell you about the snails. So far it looks like they are not reproducing."*
>
> *"I have my energy back. It is sure nice to have it. You don't realize until it is gone how good it is to have energy."*
>
> *"You two are so amazing and we have so much to be thankful for. I am sure that your job is mentally exhausting yet you give so much, and there are so many lives that you touch. Thanks for being you!"*
>
> *"You two were able to uncover a lot of things from the past in our home and release so much."*

"Joshua's health is remarkably better. No one gets creeped out anymore. We used to have the hair on the back of our necks stand up when we would go thru the basement hallway. Joshua no longer has an odor in his room. The cupboard under the old kitchen sink is no longer cold. We have to put our pop in the refrigerator now. No more strange sounds in the house. No more sightings of ghosts. We no longer have strange unexplained things such as the TV turning on or off with no one in the room. No more sounds of someone being upstairs walking around when we knew no one was up there."

"We are very happy in our home, and it didn't used to be that way.

Thanks for all that you two did for our home and our family."

Allison

Got Ghosts???

6
Shove-Ins...
The Universal Squatters

Knock, Knock...Who's There?

"Why am I being so destructive to myself and the people closest to me?" "I don't recognize what comes out of my mouth now." "All I want to do is drink and drink and drink." "Sometimes I don't even know who I am anymore." "Horrible thoughts go round and round in my head. I just can't control them or myself." If any of these thoughts are familiar to you, you just might have what we call a Shove-In.

You may have heard of the term, Walk-In. In this situation, an agreement is made between the resident being or original soul and a new soul that is choosing to take over the physical body when the original soul is finished with it. There is full consent, and a mutually agreeable spiritual contract is being honored. This is a completely different type of event than a Shove-In.

Shoving-in is a phenomenon that can occur when a person is: Knocked out or rendered unconscious; sedated; drugged up; in an alcoholic stupor; traumatized; anesthetized; under extreme stress or critically ill. All of these conditions can make someone vulnerable, weakened, or off guard, and when this happens, you have a situation that can allow an uninvited guest to literally shove into your body.

Shove-Ins are self-absorbed, opportunistic beings who are hanging around the planet in lower dimensions, waiting to find a body to get back into. There are different degrees of this phenomenon, and in extreme cases, the resident being is barely present to run the affairs of their own body. Some people might interpret this as a "Spirit Possession" or even a "Demon Possession," but we prefer to be less dramatic, more practical or matter-of-fact about it all, and simply refer to it as a Shove-In.

NOTE: *The word* **Shove-In** *is an original term inspired by Laura Lee to accurately describe this phenomenon that she sees in her healing work. For more information, read Laura Lee's book,* **Living in an Indigo House**...

Here is an extraordinary story of a Shove-In situation. No one would have dared to believe there could be a "happily ever after" in this circumstance. This is the first Shove-In eviction we participated in together.

Belligerent Brother?...
Nope, It's a Couple of Hostile Shove-Ins!

Ronnie's client Kathy had come to her for a reading, when some extraordinary information was revealed. These are Kathy's words to describe what took place.

> *For years, the brother I knew and loved had been gone. In his place was a vile insulting creature. We were close growing up and then something changed. He suddenly had so much hate and darkness in him. He was very touchy, and would fly off the handle spouting obscenities that made any family gathering tense to the point of being unbearable. When he visited our mother in the town where she and I lived, I would try to stay away from him as much as possible. I couldn't remember the last time we met that it didn't include hateful remarks. His hatefulness touched everyone he came in contact with. He had turned into an excessive*

drinker and had even gone so far as to insult his commanding officer's wife. My mother and I blamed the drinking for his change in personality and figured there was nothing we could do about it. There was no communicating with him.

My grandmother passed away in May of 2002. We were especially close and I was worried about her passing. I had called Ronnie to "check" on her for me since I knew she could communicate with the other side. At one point during the reading, my grandmother expressed a concern for my brother, Bob. Ronnie didn't even know I had a brother. Grandma told Ronnie that Bob had been involved in a car wreck and had hurt his head. She was worried about him because he wasn't doing well.

When Ronnie then tuned into my brother, she discovered that he had at least one entity that had shoved-in while he was in a vulnerable state. I vaguely remembered something about an accident, but didn't know any details. I only knew that my brother was indeed having severe personality problems. His daughter was only a few months old, and he didn't want anything to do with her. In fact he would almost get violent whenever we tried to talk about her.

After the reading with Ronnie, I spoke to my mother, and she confirmed that there had been a car wreck when Bob was about nineteen. She didn't know the details because it happened in another state. She did know that he must have suffered some type of head trauma because he now had a visible scar line on his head where hair no longer grew. Mom had asked him about it, but he didn't want to discuss it. We began to realize that it was around that time he had started to change. My mother thought it was due to drinking and living around unsavory people.

I called Ronnie for a consultation and she and Laura Lee removed the intruding entities. I cannot tell you *how grateful my family is, because not long after they did their work, my brother began to change for the better. He knows nothing about the possession or the subsequent clearing. But the difference is amazing. He is himself again! He's funny and kind. He remembers very little about the past eight years. He doesn't remember much of the hurtful times. He attributes it to the drinking. The thing is, he was sober at least half of the time. The best thing of all is that now he acknowledges his daughter and loves to spend time with her.*

The last time I saw him, before the clearing he was very thin. He was not able to eat nor was he able to sleep. His nights were filled with terrifying nightmares. He has since gained weight. He's able to sleep and is generally healthy in mind, body and spirit. He is able to drink a few beers and leave it at that without getting mean, so his personality change had nothing to do with alcohol. He used to scowl constantly now he has a bright smile. Best of all he loves me again. We talk at least two or three times a week and we always end our conversations with, "I Love You." I have my brother back. My eyes are welled with tears and my heart is filled with gratitude even as I write this today.

Thanks, Ghostbuster Gals!

Ronnie recalls the experience this way:

Kathy came to me to see if I could contact her grandmother who had recently passed. Grandma came through very quickly. A few minutes into the "conversation" however, Grandma was showing a great amount of concern for a young man that felt to be someone close to Kathy. She was very upset about this young man and showed me a vision of an accident resulting in a head injury that had changed his life in a detrimental way. Grandma wanted to make us aware that this man needed help. I questioned Kathy to see if she had a younger brother that might have a problem, and she told me about her brother Bob. She barely remembered that years ago, he was involved in some kind of mishap, but the particulars were hazy. It seems there had been an estrangement between Bob and his family not long after the accident. I felt very strongly that we had a Shove-In situation.

Kathy discussed helping her brother with her mother, then Laura Lee and I set up a time to facilitate liberating Bob of the negative entities that were corrupting his life. The first thing we did was ask permission of Bob's soul to do this work. (Believe it or not, sometimes the soul will say no, because there is more growing to be done from the experiences that are occurring.) Once we got the go-ahead we had a phone consultation with Kathy and her mom to get a little more background. After that, Laura Lee and I prepared the room and ourselves using candles, incense and sage. Moving into separate rooms, we performed our individual prayers and meditations for about half an hour.

When we rejoined each other, what a remarkable tale there was to tell. We were able to determine the stories of two entities that had attached themselves to Bob during the trauma that occurred from his accident. Some of the information we received was exactly the same, and sometimes we each got different pieces of the puzzle. We knew there was a lot of work to be done. However, before we were able to contact the two intruders, we had both noticed there was another group of three entities that had taken a special interest in the insanity that was going on. They had affixed themselves to Bob's aura for their own self-serving purposes.

As we tuned into this group, I was a little taken aback as I sensed the emanation of a very foreign energy. Fortunately Laura Lee, "Queen of Weird Sh!t," seemed to be very familiar with it. She immediately put a Kryahgenetics egg around the bizarre energy to quarantine it. At the same time, she put eggs around the two Shove-Ins and sedated them. Her guides and her guardians from the Dragon and Gargoyle realms were then called in for assistance. The three strange energy beings needed to be contained, then were escorted back to the *Ultra-Violet Realm*. Their final stop was the cosmic black hole for cleansing.

I tagged along psychically and watched in wonder for it was like nothing I had ever seen before. This was my first encounter with the *Ultraviolet Realm*. The colors and the energy were so extraordinarily unusual and vibrant that I just gawked in amazement, uttering monosyllabic words like, "Wow" and "cool." The atmosphere was almost palpable. It felt as though I was enveloped in the soft, gentle, caressing field of Love. There was a sense of majesty and grace, and the luminescent radiance was exquisite. However, there are no words in our language to accurately depict what I experienced. It was not only out of this world, but out of this Universe as well!

Once the three outer beings were sent packing, we could concentrate on the two Shove-Ins. As the information came to light about who these disembodied spirits were, we started to comprehend why Bob was such a mess. Both entities gained entrance during his auto accident. They were in the same general location, but were ghosts from different time periods. In his destabilized, unconscious condition, they had both taken the opportunity to hop a ride.

The first soul was a pioneer named Josef, who had come to America from Europe, looking for a better life. It was the mid 1800's. Traveling with his wife Judith Marie, and baby daughter, Katerina, they had to stop their westward journey in South Dakota, when an early winter storm set in. Fortunately, they had come across a deserted trapper's cabin, and it served to protect them from the harsh elements.

Unfortunately, Judith and the baby contracted a respiratory illness. Katerina was the first to succumb, as she was only eight months old. Josef and his wife were devastated. The worst part was that they felt so unbelievably helpless as they watched their daughter struggle for air as her lungs filled up with fluid. Finally, her color changed, and she gasped her last breath, as her parents looked on in agony, powerless to rescue their baby girl.

Not long after they buried their child in a snowy grave, Judith became more fragile as her illness progressed. She was in such despair and sorrow, it weakened her to the point where she could no longer carry on. Josef had been out hunting all day and was excited to finally be returning with sustenance. Running the last few yards to the cabin, he flung open the door with pride and enthusiasm. It was then he saw his wife on the makeshift bed lying absolutely still. His heart started pounding in his chest. "Oh my God... No!" he shouted. Bolting across the room, he shook his wife, calling out her name, "Judith... Judith!" There was no response. She had perished alone and in misery while he was away. He buried his head in her chest and sobbed, crying out, "I'm sorry. I am so sorry. It's all my fault. I should have never brought you and the baby out here." He rocked and cried, pouring out his anguish into her lifeless body.

Josef was left alone with an incredible amount of guilt, anger, and overwhelming grief. He felt responsible for the death of his family. Continuing about his daily survival he walked around as if in a daze, only half there.

Right now as I am relating this story, I have tears in my eyes, and a crushing sadness in my heart. The pictures of Josef's life again unfolded in front of me as I empathically reconnected to his emotional trauma. As mentioned earlier, it seems the link to many of the ghosts we send "home" remains and can be re-established when we bring them to mind. (It is very similar with our loved ones who have made their transition. In spirit form, they can actually travel at the speed of thought. So, if you are thinking about someone who has passed and you feel their presence, know that it is your thoughts that brought them to you.)

As I was viewing and experiencing Josef's heartache over his family's death, the information flow stopped. I had gotten the pieces of the puzzle up to here, and that's when Laura

Lee took over. She wasn't getting a lot of detail on Josef's life, but she sure had an idea about his death. She kept saying, "There's something about a bear. The word bear keeps coming up." Together we were able to ascertain the rest of the story.

One day out of desperation, Josef went out to check his bear traps during a blizzard. With his mind still on his grief, he inadvertently stepped in a trap he had set earlier. No matter how hard he tried, he couldn't pry the vicious, heavy steel jaws from his foot. In his shock, he almost laughed at his own stupidity. Unable to move, he was trapped there to die with his own thoughts of worthlessness, guilt, and rage.

As the life drained out of him, Josef continued to berate himself for his incompetence, which led to the death of his wife, his precious child, and now obviously his own. When he left his physical form, he was so overcome with the heavy emotions of anger, grief, despair and guilt, it kept him trapped...only now in the world of spirit. Josef's soul remained in that area for many, many years...that is until Bob had his auto accident.

Now that we had Josef's story in place, it was time to find out who our other squatter was. I knew it was a Native American man. However, I wasn't able to perceive from what time period. Then Laura Lee started to share the information she had received.

The Shove-In was a Métis or what was called a "Half Breed" in the 1970's. This was a time of bigoted politics that surrounded the tragedies of Wounded Knee. He was about thirty-four, and had a wife and seven-year-old daughter who was also of native blood.

At this point I was able to tune into this being a little stronger. Laura Lee then asked if I was able to ascertain his name. "What do you think, I'm some kind of psychic or something?" I replied. We both laughed. It was a joke we used often.

Shove-Ins...The Universal Squatters

I took a deep breath and said, "Running Eagle?...What kind of name is that! I've heard of Soaring Eagle, Flying Eagle, Swooping Eagle, but never Running Eagle." I questioned the information I was getting. It just didn't make sense to me.

It was then that I began to "see" the pictures of this man's life. As a young boy on the reservation in South Dakota, he had found a young eagle with a broken wing. Befriending the bird, he nursed it back to health. The damage was so severe the bird was unable to fly again, and so he would run with the boy wherever he went. They were inseparable. When it was time for the young man's naming ceremony at age twelve, the name Running Eagle was bestowed upon him.

Just after the travesty at Wounded Knee, the tension between white men and Indians grew to a frenzied pace. One evening, Running Eagle was leaving the local bar just outside the reservation when he noticed his left front tire was flat. He was full of alcohol and not in a good frame of mind to begin with. This just made matters worse. The safety of his beautiful wife and precious daughter weighed heavily on him, for the raids on the reservation were getting more fierce and out of control.

Bending down for a closer examination of his tire, Running Eagle discovered that someone had deliberately slashed it. That served to infuriate him even more. As he rose, contemplating his next move, the three white men who had sabotaged his car, crept up behind him. Before he was fully standing, the man in the middle took a full swing with the baseball bat he was wielding, and brutally bashed the inebriated Indian in the back of his head.

The blow was so forceful it killed Running Eagle instantly. As his soul left his physical form, he was in a state of shock and total confusion. Watching in bewilderment, the men viciously kicked his lifeless body, spewing vile insults and threats. He wondered why he didn't feel anything. They kept yelling at him, "Get up! Get up, you filthy bastard!" It didn't take long for the attackers to realize Running Eagle was never going to get up again. Their ambush successful, they quickly left the scene of their carnage, feeling no remorse.

Running Eagle passed away with such rage, despair, and shock within him that he became stuck in his own tracks, so to speak. His intense desire for retaliation for his unjust slaughter, his intoxication at the time of death, and his overwhelming sorrow, frustration and anger at not being able to be there for his family during this time of hate towards his people, caused Running Eagle to become "earthbound." In his grief and fury, he continued in the afterlife to "go on the war path," sucking the energy out of every low vibrational white man who visited the bar.

One evening, the squeal of tires and the scraping of metal reverberated into the energy plane that Running Eagle inhabited. It caught his attention enough that he went to investigate. When Bob, also of Native American ancestry (we found this out after the fact), had an auto accident in the same vicinity of where Running Eagle was trapped, the conditions were perfect for shoving-in.

Bob was intoxicated, so the alcohol element created a similar vibration. There was an electromagnetic energy generated from the skidding and sparks of the car when it crashed. This then created the perfect opportunity for the three agitating, ruthless parasites we sent to the *Ultra-Violet Realm*, to glom onto Bob's own electromagnetic field. We now had the perfect recipe for creating a chaos that would soon turn his world upside down.

These beings added an extra boost to make the Shoving-In process easier and permanent. Josef also took advantage of the situation. So, while Bob was in his vulnerable unconscious state, Running Eagle and Josef were both able to infiltrate themselves right into his consciousness.

The "like vibration" of pain, suffering, grief and anger made this all possible. They say, "Three's a crowd," well, that is certainly an understatement in this case! Running Eagle was on the warpath, and he now had two white men to wage war with. In this bizarre scenario, he could now drown his sorrows in booze and pick a fight with everyone he met. He could finally continue on his agenda of hostility and revenge, only now it was so much better since he had a physical body to manipulate.

Josef was also now able to vent his anger at the world that had caused such suffering. The fact that he had an Indian as a cohort did not make things any easier. You see, Indians were responsible for wiping out his younger brother as well as the rest of his family. This caused what we would now call racial anxiety.

Poor Bob didn't stand a chance when his girlfriend delivered a baby girl. Both Running Eagle and Josef in different ways suffered the loss of their adored daughters, harboring that profound pain within their souls. This birth brought up so much anguish and distress that all hell broke loose in the psyches of the Shove-Ins. Is it any wonder why Bob flew into a vile rage when his daughter was even mentioned?

So, now Laura Lee and I had our work cut out for us. Deciding which entity to remove first, we went about constructing a portal "home." Re-establishing telepathic communication, I attempted to convince Josef it was time to leave. Well, he would have none of it. He wasn't going anywhere! Laura Lee and I looked at each other in helpless frustration. What do we do now? That's when I remembered one of my first ghostbustings at the mansion when Anya had brought the parents of little Jolene back to help her cross. With that in mind, I contacted Josef's wife Judith and asked her to come through the portal to escort him "home." As soon as she appeared (holding their daughter in her arms,) Josef's whole demeanor changed. Overwhelmed and overjoyed, he softened up as tears welled in his eyes. Opening the transparent Egg, it did not take long for Josef to move out of Bob and into the tunnel. The reunion was heartwarming.

Turning our attention to Running Eagle, I realized we would have to be a little more creative since his family was probably still alive. Fortunately, I work very closely with the Angels and received some brilliant insight. I had been gifted a sacred pipe (chanupa) by a Métis Shaman. Knowing how important it is to relate to an entity on their level, I decided to take the pipe inside the Egg and smoke him out. (That is…I smoked the pipe with him.) Gaining his respect and confidence, I was able to convince Running Eagle it was time to return to "Great Spirit." Laura Lee noticed that when the egg opened, it resembled the flap of a teepee. We both thought that was very strange and yet logical. In fact, we still use the teepee idea when dealing with Native American spirits.

Taking some deep breaths, Laura Lee and I felt we were done. Bob seemed clear with his own energy intact. I wondered how long it would take to see an effect from this Shove-In removal process. My Angels then chimed in loud and clear, "You will know your work is done when he asks about his daughter."

A few days later I got a call from Kathy. She was very excited. Thanking Laura Lee and me profusely, she exclaimed, "I have my brother back! He told me he loved me on the phone, and he even asked about his daughter!"

At that moment I breathed a sigh of relief and knew we had been successful.

Months later, an interesting side note to this story occurred. During the initial reading, Kathy had inquired about her future and what her mission was. I told her that within the next two months it would all become clear. She laughed skeptically and said, "Yeah, right."

The stories of the Shove-Ins that we removed from Bob had a profound effect on Kathy. She was especially interested in the Native American aspect.

Here is the rest of the story in Kathy's own words.

Out of curiosity I chose to do some research on the name "Running Eagle" in the vicinity of where the entity that shoved in was from. I came across a man my age on death row. This man has been on death row since we were kids. While I went to college, traveled, had a family, he sat in a cell on death row. This intrigued me and I as I hit on other links, I realized this was epidemic. People living in prison, dying in prison, on their way to prison, was an epidemic! Within days I met the founder of a new non-profit organization that works with prisoners, the children of prisoners and at-risk children, to try to help them with their lives in order to avoid becoming just another statistic.

I found my passion and my mission all within the time frame Ronnie had given me. I began working with this organization and have done so now for many years. I believe that prisons are not only a breeding ground for hate and darkness but may be a breeding ground for Shove-Ins as well.

Another interesting twist to my story is that I have had nightmares of being trapped in prison since I was a child. I have been deathly afraid of prison and have never considered venturing into one, let alone contacting anyone in prison. Since I began working with prisoners my fear and the nightmares are a thing of the past.

My capacity for compassion and acceptance has grown immensely, and through it all there is one thing I know for sure; no matter what we may think we know or see, there is so much that we do not. I thank Laura Lee and Ronnie for their help with my brother and for their continued guidance when I cannot see things for myself.

Obsessive Compulsive?...
Nope, It's a Desperate Housewife!

This is a letter from one of Ronnie's clients who had no idea she had a squatter in her midst:

I came to Ronnie with questions about my life, and about this immense feeling of self-doubt, and obsessive-compulsive behavior I had had for years. Ronnie asked about the behavior, which I explained was about feeling contaminated, guilty, anxious, and terrified of hurting others. (There was a phase I went through when I would be in a kitchen and would feel terrified that I would pick up a knife and kill someone.) I obsessed about germs, and about leaving the oven on – terrified that I would cause some disaster.

Ronnie asked if I knew what a Shove-In was. She also asked if I had had any major trauma in my life, like a car accident or surgery, where I would have been unconscious. (I had surgery when I was eighteen or nineteen, and had been unconscious for it.) Ronnie explained that when a person is in this state, another spirit can shove-in.

What Ronnie saw, when she tuned into my energy, was the spirit of a woman who had committed suicide. Her name was Cynthia, and her stepfather had sexually abused her. Her mother had blamed her for it, and had made it clear to Cynthia that she was "dirty." At the time she killed herself, Cynthia was separated from her husband, had two small children and was out of work. Before her own suicide, she murdered her son and daughter, because she didn't want them to be motherless or risk the same abuse she had suffered as a child.

* **Author's note**: Cynthia stabbed her children to death with a large kitchen knife. She then turned it on herself, hacking away at the woman she loathed. She passed out before she could finish the job. One of her neighbors had heard the children screaming and called 911. Cynthia was then rushed to the hospital in an ambulance. Her injuries were so extensive, she passed away on the operating table.

Cynthia's children went to the Light, but, being very religious, she herself felt doomed to hell, and didn't go anywhere until she found me.

I told Ronnie that I had been abused sexually too. Ronnie said that Cynthia chose me because our energies resonated. We had similar vibrational frequencies.

Ronnie asked if I would like her to send Cynthia to the Light. I said yes, and Ronnie tuned in to communicate with Cynthia. She wanted to know if I forgave her, which I did. Ronnie continued to communicate with Cynthia. I wasn't actively involved in what Ronnie was doing, but I felt an emotional surge from my belly as Ronnie was in the process of removing her and sent her to the Light.

When Ronnie finished, she explained to me what happened: Jesus had come to take Cynthia home, but she was crouching in shame, and couldn't look at him. He touched her on the shoulder, and told her that where she was going there was only Love. She looked up and was bathed in pure unconditional love and acceptance. Then she went "home."

I didn't notice anything different in the way I felt right away, rather I observed things gradually over the next few days. The first thing I noticed was that my posture was better – when I got in my truck to leave Ronnie's, I noticed that I was sitting straighter, and that it was easier for me to sit up straight.

*The next morning, I woke up **not** feeling distraught and anxious, as I often did. Many mornings I would wake up with a great deal of anxiety, and it would take some time to become clear, to step out of what felt like "static."*

I feel clearer in general, less burdened. A depression has lifted. I am standing straighter, walking taller, with head and eyes up. It's easier to breathe deeply. I feel more confident and centered. Irritation has lifted.

I'm not feeling overwhelmed with guilt and anxiety anymore. There is an absence of negative self-talk and self-pity. I'm not beating myself up. Shame has lifted. I'm not making anxiety-laden mountains out of molehills. Over-the-top perfectionism has lifted. My perspective is more in balance. I still find myself doing some of the behaviors I did obsessively, but they are not loaded with fear, guilt and anxiety. (As Ronnie said, I might still do them, but they'll be more like habits without the emotional charge.)

I'm continuing to notice changes. I feel like my brain is adjusting to these new conditions. I was noticing yesterday that I'm having an easier time speaking. It's easier to articulate what I'm thinking and feeling – it just flows better. I feel very grateful!

Thank you.

Split Personality?...
Nope, It's Two Nasty Shove-Ins!

This story is told by Maurah, one of Laura Lee's clients who had been plagued to the max throughout her life with Shove-Ins. When Maurah came to her for help, she suspected her brother Tom had a Shove-In. Laura Lee had no prior information on her brother, except that he was mean to Maurah as a child. The similarities between the personalities of the Shove-Ins and Maurah's brother were quite amazing, as you will see for yourself.

> *Throughout my life I have been inundated by people who had Shove-Ins. At one time, about eighty percent of the people around me had them! As a child and as an adolescent, every single person in my nuclear family had Shove-Ins. Later, my husband, one son, three daughters-in-law, and a grandson all had Shove-Ins. Even the "friends" who surrounded me had them. It was as though I had a magnet on my forehead that read, "Shove-Ins Welcome Here."*
>
> *The focus of my story will be on the Shove-Ins of my older brother Tom, who had two of them. The first one Laura Lee detected, infiltrated when he was nine, and the second one came in at age eighteen. Based upon his malevolent behavior toward me, as his younger sister, you will see how vicious his first Shove-In truly was.*
>
> *As very young children (before Tom's Shove-In invaded), he was sweet and protective of his little sis. We got along very well, and I trusted him. After his Shove-In took over, he dramatically changed and became very hostile toward me. He became physically, emotionally and psychologically abusive. Tom was extremely jealous of the attention our father bestowed upon me.*

Our father, who also had a Shove-In affecting him, found fault with Tom throughout his life, and made it clear that I was his favorite. Nothing Tom did was ever right, and he often received beatings with a belt. My mother, who was infested with a cross-dressing gay man Shove-In, preferred Tom. The family dynamics that were produced as a result of the many different personalities involved, created pure dysfunction, jealousy, confusion and even hatred among the members.

The problem with Shove-Ins is that the underlying core person, or true self, may be kind and loving and act accordingly, but then for no apparent reason, their behavior changes as the Shove-In activates. This creates mistrust and confusion for someone who is in a relationship with this split-personality type being. I was bombarded by these schizophrenic personalities continually.

When Tom was around nine years old, he became violent; hitting me, knocking me down stairs, breaking my storybook porcelain dolls, and constantly making fun of me. I remember being locked in an attic by him for what seemed like hours. He also locked me out of the house, chasing me around and shooting at me with his BB gun, scaring me half to death. We were latchkey kids so we were often left alone, and hence, had little parental supervision or protection.

Another time Tom socked me in the stomach as hard as he could. (As an adult, I discovered I had a hernia from that blow.) Our father beat him for it. This just seemed to make Tom all the more determined to get back at me.

Growing up on a lake created a backdrop for some dangerous Shove-In misadventures. As adolescents we played a game called, "King of the Raft." We'd jump from the raft, which was anchored in deep water, and see who could hold their breath the longest while

Shove-Ins... The Universal Squatters

submerged under the water. That person would be, "King of the Raft." Tom had strong lungs. I on the other hand did not, as I suffered from bi-lateral pneumonia as a baby. On one occasion, I remember that I expended extra effort to stay under water as long as possible, and when I came up, gasping for air, Tom pushed me back under, trying to drown me. Were it not for another friend who had intervened, he would have succeeded.

As an adult, Tom became violent with his wife and I suspect his daughters were victims of abuse as well. Once, after my own divorce, when he knew I was alone in my house, he came over in a drunken stupor, kissed me on the mouth and announced that he was going to commit incest with me. He was over two hundred pounds and very strong, so he could have easily overpowered me. I quickly outmaneuvered him, and started to call his wife on the phone telling him, "No you aren't, I'm calling your wife right now to tell her you're here." He finally left.

I always wanted a healthy relationship with Tom, (he is my only sibling), but that was impossible while he was afflicted with the invasion of the body snatchers.

Recently Laura Lee removed both of Tom's Shove-Ins and here are their stories:

The first Shove-In, Renaul, gained access when Tom was nine. During a Little League game, he was hit by a baseball bat, and lost consciousness. Renaul Vandure, the ghost that shoved-in, died in 1915 at the age of twenty-six. His father was very abusive and beat him with a horsewhip. (Tom's father used a leather belt.) Renaul was an only child and was very close to his mother. She tried to protect him, but she passed away when he was only nine. It devastated him, as he loved her very much. (Tom always preferred and loved his mom.) Now, it was just he and his dad.

When Renaul was fourteen, he and his father got into a fight, which resulted in a knocked out front tooth. (Tom had a front tooth knocked out playing sports.) Renaul left home after that. He got a job at a metal smelting plant and worked there for eight years.

After Renaul had been at his job for about three years, he was involved in an accident, and received horrible burns on his face, neck and arm. He didn't die, but he was scarred for life. He became a hideous "Scarface" with a missing front tooth. It humiliated him and altered the rest of his life. Women and children were afraid of him, and turned away when they saw him approaching.

Just before Renault's disfiguring accident he had a casual relationship with a young woman that resulted in a pregnancy. The child was born after the life changing disaster, and the woman came to Renaul for financial support. Renaul denied the boy was his, but inside knew otherwise. He didn't want his son to know that he was his father because he was ashamed of his grotesque appearance.

Renaul left the smelting plant at the age of twenty-two and being a big burly guy who was very intimidating, got a job with a loan shark. He frightened people into paying, and beat them up if necessary. He eventually became a killer-for-hire, having no compunction in taking a life.

Renaul then developed Rheumatic fever, became delirious and died. (Tom also had rheumatic fever.) Guilt and anger about his sordid life kept him trapped. He eventually realized he was a ghost.

Renaul shoved into Tom because he reminded him of the son he denied, who would have been about that age when he passed. He tried to live his life through Tom and was instrumental in getting him into drinking. Renaul had a distain for women because after the accident that left him scarred, no woman would have anything to do with him. (Tom mistreated women.)

Laura Lee put Renaul in a Kryahgenetics Egg, which freaked him out at first because he was not used to being confined. Then he put his hands on the egg and watched like he was looking out a window. As the Egg floated up and onto the opening of the portal, two angels were awaiting.

Renaul said, "I'm not going in there!" Laura Lee explained to him that he was dead and he needed to go. He folded his arms and said, "**No, I'm staying right here!**" Then he saw a black dog coming down the portal. It was Pal... the only real friend he ever had. Renaul looked at the dog in disbelief, and was now excited to go. The Egg opened, and Pal came bounding down the tunnel to meet him. Renaul was thrilled! He smiled and sobbed as he hugged his dog. He turned and said, "Tell whoever helped me see Pal, thank you." Then he walked through the tunnel with Pal as the angels escorted him to his life review.

Tom's second shove-in penetrated his being when he was eighteen years old, passed out, drunk. His name was Chip Gregerson, and he was attracted by Tom's drinking. Chip died at the age of twenty, while he was driving drunk. Chip was very nice looking and had a job as a delivery man. Women found him very attractive. He had a nice build and magnetic appeal. (Tom displayed some of Chip's charisma.) Chip needed to be right, in control, and appeared to have it all together.

There was a lot of discord inside Tom, as his two Shove-Ins were always at odds with each other. Renaul hated "pretty boy Chip," and they were constantly fighting for control of the body. This caused a lot of the craziness in Tom's head. The only thing they could agree on was alcohol.

Laura Lee egged Chip and placed him on the portal doorway. Chip looked around and seemed confused. Then he saw his grandmother who looked remarkably like his own mother, coming down the tunnel, surrounded by angels. He didn't really believe in angels, but he was okay with them at that moment. His grandmother held out his pet turtle that was crushed by a car when he was young. This had devastated him.

After that, Chip was secretly fearful of death, and passed that perception on to Tom. Chip was amazed and thrilled at everything that was happening, and walked through the tunnel holding his turtle. Then he turned and waved as if to say, "Thank you," and the portal closed.

After having both Shove-Ins removed, Tom's behavior has totally changed. He never makes fun of me anymore. He speaks to me with respect, and does the same with his new wife. He is much more loving, and is even doing yoga with his new wife. Tom has become a sweet, gentle man—the man he was intended to be before he was hijacked by the Shove-Ins.

The most important attitude transformation I have witnessed was Tom's willingness and enthusiasm to help me set up Aulmauracite grids in the downtown Detroit and Belle Isle area. (See Chapter 10 for more details about grids.) Tom was my knight and protector during this mission, without any ulterior motives. After all these years, I finally have the brother I have always wanted!

~ ~ ~ ~ ~

These are just a sampling of the many Shove-In removals we have handled. You can now understand how detrimental and even life-threatening it can be to have unknown intruders sharing space and controlling someone's being.

When there are Shove-In's present, personalities and demeanor can change suddenly and dramatically. It can be quite frustrating and confusing for those who are the closest. In our opinion, it may even be the reason why divorce rates, abuse, alcoholisms, drug use, and violent crimes are running rampant.

Most of the beings that shove in feed on negativity and fear. They hijack someone else's body and try to continue their dysfunctional behaviors. If you suspect that someone in your life has a Shove-In, you may now understand the reason behind all the insanity.

We tell our clients that "Time Shares" might be an enjoyable experience if you're talking about vacation condos, but it's a "hell-uv-a" way to run a body!

Got Ghosts???

Synchronicity...
What are the Odds?

And Other W.S.

Most of us have experienced incidents of synchronicity whether we believe in it or not. Some people call these coincidences. In our world, there is no such thing.

Here in Ronnie's words are a few examples of how synchronicity has worked in her life. You may have some examples of your own.

There are times that even though Laura Lee and I live about thirty minutes apart, we don't see each other for months. During the summer of 2007, we had been trying to connect for quite a few weeks and just kept missing one another.

I needed to leave for a short trip, and I figured I would catch Laura Lee after I returned. I was heading for San Francisco to teach a Twilight Brigade/Compassion in Action training. I arrived at the airport a little early because I was flying Southwest and needed to get in line to get a good seat. However, by the time I got there, the line was already into the aisle and was a jumbled mess.

As I tried to determine which row was A, B, or C, I looked down at a woman sitting on the floor to see if I could get a peek at the letter on her boarding pass so I would know what line to stand in. Imagine my surprise when I saw the name Mistycah on the paper! Without realizing it, Laura Lee and I were flying on the same plane. Now, what are the odds?

Synchronicities occur all the time, if we pay attention. I look at it as the Universe's way of saying, "Hi, just wanted to let you know you're on track" or "You are right where you need to be." or, "Remember, thoughts can and do create reality." It brings me a sense of delight and wonderment at the perfection.
(So, what are your thoughts right now?)

Sometimes the synchronicities are just small things like:

- ~ I had just typed my husband's name in an email and a few seconds later he called on the phone. I can't tell you how many times whether I'm traveling, or in town, we'll start to call each other at the exact same moment. When he's at work, I'll think of him and he'll call.

- ~ I sent an email to my friend Aaron, and he called one minute later (before he ever received it).

- ~ Invariably whenever I have contact with Laura Lee, whether it's through email, live on the phone, or I need to leave her message, the number 55 is somehow involved. There are so many instances when I have jumped up, grabbed the phone because I felt the need to call her, and then glanced at the clock and it's 5:55. (That's her spirit guide Hal's code number.) As I was going through a final edit of this chapter, when I got to this paragraph, I happened to look at the time and it was 10:55. Now what are the odds?

- ~ As for my special numbers, I will see 10:06 on the clock a great deal of the time. Why is this significant? My birthday is October 6th. It makes me smile and I feel as though my Angels are saying, "Happy Birthday!"

~ Another number that holds a special importance for me is the Angel number 444. I cannot tell you how many times I'll wake up, turn to look at the clock and it's 4:44. In fact it happened just last night as well. It's interesting to note I met a very special friend, *New York Times* bestselling author, G.W. Hardin (*The Messengers*) because of 444.

~ While talking on the phone one afternoon, I mentioned my friend Aaron, and a few minutes later, a call came in. You guessed it, his name was on the caller ID. This has happened with him numerous times since he is a very perceptive Indigo.

~ Immediately after I finished addressing an envelope at 10:30 pm, the person I was sending the letter to, called on the phone.

~ Laura Lee and I were working on the book together and I asked her if we should include a story about a Shove-In removal we did for an old friend of ours. Neither of us had seen or heard from this person in over four years. Less than an hour later, an email alert showed up on Laura Lee's computer and it was from this person! What are the odds?

~ I was looking through some papers on my desk and came across a business card of a client I hadn't seen or spoken to in three years. She is a Naturopathic Doctor and I have some fond memories of the work we had done together. I knew she moved to Oregon and had gotten married. Two days after I looked at her card, I received a phone call from her. She and her mother (also a client of mine) wanted to come for readings. They drove all the way from Oregon specifically for that purpose.

~ As I was writing the story in chapter two about the TV reporter and cameraman, I just typed that last word when an email came in from Kirk, the cameraman.

~ While working on chapter eight, Ghosts' Stories, I went to check something on the Internet. Yahoo is my home page, and the first thing I saw was a headline that said, "Who ya gonna call?" There was a story about the old Ghostbusters movie. What are the odds?

~ I was sending Laura Lee an email, using my Outlook account, which only needs me to type the first few letters, and the address will come up. For some strange reason as I typed the "L," the address for Lorraine, a client I have not spoken to in years, popped up. A fond thought or two passed through my mind as I continued my endeavor to email Laura Lee. A few minutes later the phone rang. Yes, of course, it was Lorraine, but she didn't even realize it was me she was calling. She asked for Ronnie with some other last name. When I told her which Ronnie I was, she was shocked. She said that someone had given her the name and number of a really good psychic, and Lorraine had no idea she was calling me. Now, how weird is that?

Speaking of weird, even though Laura Lee is the "Queen of Weird Sh!t," I do have a story of my own.

Four years ago, I received a digital camera for Christmas. I have taken hundreds of pictures and video with it and I always download the data to my computer and erase the card.

This year for my birthday, my wonderful husband gave me a new camera with better video capabilities. So, I started using the new one.

As I went to bed one night, I was thinking about my old horse, Joe. He was thirty-five when we had to put him down. I was feeling guilty because the last few months of his life seemed to be a living hell.

Thinking he was lonely, I had bought a couple more horses to keep him company. Well, since he was such a kind and gentle soul, they did nothing but pick on him. His body was ravaged with bite marks.

As I fell asleep, I wondered about Joe and how he felt about being ostracized by his own kind. I also missed him terribly.

The next morning after we had almost two feet of snow, the sun was out, radiantly sparkling on a carpet of white. It looked like a winter wonderland, so I grabbed both my cameras and started taking pictures.

Later that afternoon I downloaded both cameras to my computer. The first things that showed up from my old camera were four old videos of Joe! Now, I had taken pictures and videos, downloaded them and erased the card on that camera consistently for three years after those Joe videos had been taken. So, I cannot for the life of me figure out how those four videos appeared in front of the new pictures I took that day.

If you can figure it out, please let me know.

These are just a few of the many synchronistic events that have occurred within the last year or so. It's important to remember that the Universe (God, Angels, guides, loved ones, ghosts) communicates with us in many different languages. Sometimes it's through the lyrics of a song, sometimes through numbers as you have seen, or sometimes even through animals, as each animal we encounter has a message of its own. All we need to do is pay attention and open our minds and hearts.

It's About Time

Laura Lee had a problem with clocks. Clocks in her house would suddenly jump forward or backward in time, then stop completely for no reason. Even her wristwatch would jump ahead. To her disbelief, she also witnessed one of her clock's second hand literally run backwards...which would be *counterclockwise*. It was like time was "out of time" for her in every respect.

On a spiritual journey to the pyramids in Mexico, unbeknownst to Laura Lee, she showed up exceptionally early to meet a group for ceremonial preparations. Of course, no one was around. Walking up and down the ancient roads, she was totally confused, and wondered where everyone was. Since her watch had been fine all day, it took her a while to figure out that this watch was suddenly, "out of time," and she had arrived over an hour early! (Now, you need to understand that being on time used to be an extreme challenge for her.) She was mystified, but attributed it to the intense energy surrounding the women's ceremony she was about to conduct on top of a pyramid.

Laura Lee has had lots of W.S. surrounding other electronic devices. It has become a very normal part of her life. For instance, her TV and computer used to turn off all of a sudden, but the rest of the power in the house stayed on...and it did **not** flip a circuit breaker!

This one is interesting. The fax phone would ring without being plugged into the phone jack! When this happened on her birthday at 7:20 p.m., (the exact time she was born), she figured it was Hal, her esoteric guide. She also used to get pop up error messages on her computer with notes from Hal.

We've included a couple of Hal's messages so you can get an idea of how weird her W.S. really was.

At 1:55 p.m. "We need to talk, the Light is here, and it's yours."

"It's your Hal. It's Hal time........{ YEA.... :) " When Laura Lee looked at her computer it was 11:55 p.m.

Anti-Synchronicity and Other W.S. A Sad But True Tale by Laura Lee

We have all heard wonderful, amazing stories about how people and things seem to accidentally come together perfectly or magically fall into place. This is called being in the flow, or being in sync.

There is a flip side to this, however, that I can bear witness to. Many people believe that if you just think positive thoughts and put out good intent, that your life will always be full of wonderful things. This is possible, and I am a great advocate of a positive mental attitude. Change your mind and you change your life. There are incidents nevertheless, that have nothing to do with how positive your thinking is, and everything to do with unseen forces.

I have a firm conviction of spiritual contracts here on planet Earth, and that many of us experience some very hostile environments in order to educate ourselves to fulfill our personal agreements. First Wave Indigos are a classic example of putting themselves in harm's way to survive very negative, even life threatening situations in order to get the education they need to change the world. You don't fully understand the darkness unless you have experienced it, and you can't change something you don't know anything about.

I must have foolishly volunteered for more than my share of intense spiritual contracts, because I had found myself in many situations that my logical mind told me, "Stay the heck away from there! I have a very baaaaad feeling about this!" Then my spirit guides defy this good common sense and say, "Go ahead, do it. You need the experience."

Marrying my second husband, Robert was one such contract. My entire fleet of internal red flags were raised when I met him, and I knew that underneath the charisma and good sense of humor, were some extremely arrogant and self-serving roots. He was a master at Native American shamanism, and could manipulate people and things with his magick. I observed it all and realized that he really enjoyed the promise of this kind of power.

Robert had a huge following of people that darned near worshiped him. This was appalling to me. Those who were close to him though, soon realized he had mood swings that could give you a whip lash trying to follow them. I would try to make light of it and tell him, "Take your yellow jacket off and put your stinger away," to mellow him out. Sometimes it would work, and sometimes it made him worse.

It seemed like I was living with more than one person most of the time, and I never knew who would come out next and when. Everyday was a crapshoot. I questioned my decision to marry him constantly. More pain and sorrow were endured during those four years with him, and I cried more in that span of time, than I did in my entire life...including when I was a baby!

The wealth of information I received from living with Robert though was worth several PhD's. The reason for his personality swings, I discovered, was not that he had multiple personalities within him, but multiple people! There were five beings inhabiting that body and the three tyrannical ones would use the two nice ones to schmooze people so he could take advantage of them. Once I figured this out, I explained it to him, and gave him the opportunity to let me help take the Shove-Ins out. However, his arrogance (and the nasty buggers inside) ungracefully declined, meaning there was a lot of swearing involved. This was the last straw for me and we became estranged shortly after this discussion. I did my best for four years, and finally my spirit guides gave me the thumbs up to leave.

After the split, strange things would take place all the time. I mean stranger than was normal for me. For one thing, a day or two after he left, I woke up early in the morning before the kids got up and smelled coffee and cigarettes. I immediately thought, "Shoot, he's **back**!" Nervously, I leaped out of bed to check the coffeemaker, and to my surprise, it was empty! I sniffed through the house and the odors would phase in and phase out. I checked the patio where he always went to smoke, drink coffee and do business on the phone. It was empty except for the dogs in the back yard. The fumes of the cigarettes I had anticipated were not there. Then I thought, *"Dang, are the kids in the basement smoking behind my back?"*

I ran downstairs expecting to see them perched by the window puffing on a cigarette, but my apprehension was alleviated when I opened the door, and they were all sleeping soundly. Heading back upstairs, I checked the front yard. No one was there, and neither were any of his vehicles. Frustrated, I went back to my room. The smells were still present, but were now way more intense. This made me realize that Robert was, for whatever reason, projecting himself back into the house, especially my bedroom!

I also felt various types of hostile energy bombarding my home and my being. It seemed that this energy wanted me to either wither up and die, or make me come crawling back to my ex and grovel. Fat chance!

Another very strange thing happened that was not only out of time, but out of space as well. I was getting my things ready to do medical intuitive readings at a psychic fair, when my daughter came running into the house and yelled, "Mom, you have got to come outside and see this!" I was rushing around and already late, but she insisted, so I grabbed some of the boxes I needed to take anyway, and went outside to see what all the drama was about. She pointed to the sky above the driveway and said, "**Look!**" I could not believe my eyes. **Huge** flakes of snow were falling on what seemed to be just my yard, and immediate surroundings. There were no clouds in the sky, except for some way off on the horizon in the opposite direction from where the wind was coming. These snow fakes were literally falling from blue skies! I knew it was some kind of sign, but didn't know what it meant, except that it was some R.W.S!

You have heard of things going from "bad to worse," well, in my case it went from "bad to mega bad!"

I only had three or four months of partial respite before I got tangled up with, and immersed in my next contract, who I will call, "LQ." He was the son of a b!tch and an evil Cult Lord. In my efforts to help him break free from this extremely sinister, perverted, foul, mind controlling cult, and break away from his evil family, I found myself losing all my resources, and ending up homeless for the third time in my life.

I was devastated and scared to the core. It broke my heart when I had to send the dogs to the pound, and my kids to go live with their dad and stepmother...who did **not** want them. I had every anti-synchronicity you can imagine descending upon me, but thanks to the kindness of Ronnie, I ended up inhabiting her basement for nearly a year. She can attest to the mind boggling, logic defying, horrific things that occurred. I seemed to be inundated by Murphy's Law, except even Murphy's Law was not as bad as this!

My computer, online accounts, and website were hacked on a regular basis. When the server tried to find the culprit, they always came up empty handed. I was the only one with the pass codes, as I was my own web master. I finally changed servers thinking this would help. It took not just a few days as one would expect, but more than a month of aggravation to finally get up and running again! With the new server, new things happened, and somehow my pass codes got mysteriously changed, locking me out of my accounts nearly every other month...and, no one in the office could tell me why. I had problems with just about anything I tried to do to correct this.

I put an ad in the paper for a new business I started, and a simple ten line add turned into a nightmare of crazy events. All they had to do was cut and paste the ad...a no-brainer. They sent me back the proof and several things had been altered and changed from how I had given it to them. I sent it back corrected, and it happened again and again. When it finally came out in the newspaper, they had printed the wrong phone number! Someone else received all my calls, and she was **not** a happy camper about it! I asked the ad agent if she always had this much trouble. She said, **"Never!"** By the time the ad was placed with the correct phone number, even after proofing it, they screwed up the email and web address. As a result, the response was minimal compared to what it could have been.

Another bizarre thing happened. Much of the time it seemed like I was utterly invisible. No one who was looking for me or my services, could seem to find me. If I did psychic fairs, I would get stuck in a dark corner where there was no traffic, or even if I had a good spot, people would just walk by as if I wasn't there. Sometimes they would literally veer off to the opposite side of the room like an invisible force had pushed them away.

I called an old friend who said she had been trying to locate me for over a year and couldn't find me even though my web and email address had stayed the same.

I really knew something was wrong when I went into a store and the clerks would wait on everyone but me...and there I was standing right in front of them! Now this invisibility shield only worked for people I needed to connect with. When I wanted to be invisible, wham, a neon spotlight was on me.

An example of how this invisibility curse worked is when I scraped together twenty-five dollars so I could buy my son, Xavier some new shoes. I borrowed a car from his dad, since my car was broken down...again. My ex then told me to be careful because the license plate tags have expired. I had no choice but to take the car, my son's shoes had big holes in them, and school was starting the next day. Well, I was about halfway to the store, and as you may have guessed, I was spotted by a policeman who proceeded to pull me over.

I told the officer that I was sure I wasn't speeding and he replied, "No, you weren't, but your tags have expired." He then slapped me with a six hundred and fifty dollar fine for the tags and no proof of insurance. This mission of mercy set me back tremendously, since being invisible also made my income nearly nonexistent at that time.

I know for a fact that I had so many curses, voodoo doo-doo, whammies and black magick spells on me it was beyond a joke, even though I tried to laugh about it. These were perpetrated upon me not only from my ex, Robert, but also LQ's family who didn't want me meddling in their sordid "family affairs"... and I mean this literally!

I needed help desperately and one of Ronnie's shaman friends offered to assist me energetically. I was very grateful as he and his wife agreed to come to Ronnie's house and barter energetic healing. I was a little concerned for them, but they felt confident and were willing to help. I desperately needed it, so an appointment was set.

The session was wonderful, and I thought that maybe things would lighten up, that maybe this was the turning point. Well, things did indeed turn, but not in the direction I had hoped. I found out a couple of days later that on their way home, the healers ran off the road and nearly went down a steep embankment, but fortunately a tree had stopped them. Their car was totaled!

I felt horrible. I knew that it was no accident, but was grateful for the protection that they did have by hitting the tree...if you call that protection. The whole thing was just too coincidental to brush away as a fluke. I crawled into my shell after that and decided I should just figure out how to untangle from this mess by myself instead of getting innocent people involved.

I got so frustrated because it seemed as if it didn't matter how hard I worked, or how much psychic effort and positive intent I put into turning my life around, the results were always the same. So, I figured I might as well not even get out of bed in the morning since nothing would get accomplished anyway.

I started doing three and five card tarot spreads, attempting to get some inspiration on how to break out of this mess. Nine times out of ten, I would draw either the Hanged Man or the Death Card, or both! The deck had seventy-eight cards! So, you tell me, what are the odds? I considered this to be synchronicity, slapping me in the face as a reminder of exactly how accursed my life was!

My daughter, Ma' Lady was a real support for me and tried to keep my spirits up with her cheery attitude and funny retorts. One day we were doing a tarot spread together and she said, "Mommy, why don't you take out the Hanged Man and the Death Card right now and just get it over with. I laughed so hard I about choked. She was right!

Things got so bad that when I woke up in the morning my first thoughts were, *"Oh sssh!t, I'm alive, I'm still on planet Earth, and still in the middle of this nightmare."*

It was midsummer and Ronnie was about to move into her new house in the woods. Somehow I scraped up enough money to get a small apartment for me and the kids. Then the unthinkable happened. LQ came to live with us. At that time I was clueless as to the upheaval this man would create in my life.

W.S. and R.W.S.S. now took on new meaning. Everything around us was breaking or getting stuck. My computer was constantly in the shop, and the techie would just shake his head when he saw us coming. The inexplicable seemed to be the norm.

One time as the computer was booting up, LQ said, "Hurry, come and see this!" At the bottom of the computer screen on the bios page, there was a personal message to me. It said, "Laura Lee, if you do *it*, (I was preparing to clear a specific cult program from LQ's head, compliments of his evil dad), your computer will die. We See You!" Well, I am tenacious enough not to let bizarre computer threats intimidate me, so I went ahead and removed the program from LQ, and a few days later, my computer crashed and it did indeed die. I lost a lot of important data, which set me back even further.

During this anti-synchronistic time, other interesting phenomena happened. Every single time I was on a radio show, there were **always** technical difficulties! On one show the transmitters went out right before I was supposed to be on the air. During another show the volume kept fluctuating for no apparent reason, driving the engineer nuts. At one point during a different show, I was just starting to talk about a really important W.S. topic and I got cut off the air. Poof, I was gone! They finally got me back just in time for the show to end. The host said that this had never happened on his show before, and later he told me it has never happened since.

These kinds of electromagnetic glitches went on and on and on. It got so bad that even when I would go to buy something at a store, the computers on their cash register would act up.

Anything that had to do with my vehicle was a nightmare. Early one dark, rainy evening when returning from teaching a class in Canada, the distributor kept short-circuiting. LQ would have to go out with a flashlight and hit the distributor with a wrench while I tried to start it up again. This happened so many times I lost track after fifty. Navigating through many winding, deserted roads, what should have been a three-hour trip took over five hours to get home.

We finally got a new distributor from the scrap yard and it ran quite well after that. However, one afternoon while taking a drive on the highway, I started thinking about how nice it was that the car had been doing so well. In fact, since we got the new distributor, it hadn't cut out on us again, and actually ran without any incidents. I started feeling really grateful so I instinctively patted the dashboard and said, "You are such a good little car, you have been doing so well lately, I'm really proud of you. Thank you for being such a good car."

I immediately got the feeling that I shouldn't have done that...it was like I had jinxed it or something. Sure enough, within a half a minute of my little burst of gratitude, the car started sputtering and choking so badly that I had to pull over...and then it died.

I tried and tried to get it started again with no luck. Then I thought, "*Hmmm, maybe things had gotten so bass-ackwards, that good is bad, and bad is good. Maybe I need to try something different.*" With that thought, I smacked the dashboard and yelled, "You worthless piece of crap car, you're toast! When I get you back to town I'm calling the scrap yard to come and pick you up, and take you to the crusher! You're nothing but a big pile of junk!" I then made another attempt at starting the car, still dissing it, and this time...it started right up! I never had a problem since.

The drama continued, and I now know why all the odds were against me. You may understand when you hear the rest of this tale.

Helping LQ had darned near killed me on several occasions. He was like a black hole sucking dry every resource I had. I felt eternally trapped because I was forced into a situation where I was with him literally twenty-four-seven in very cramped quarters. I had been locked into circumstances that without some financial backing, I could not get LQ out of my house. I was in survival mode each and every day, so it felt like I was in a perpetual trap. There was also a very real threat of having all sorts of governmental agencies on my tail because of him, since LQ was an illegal alien. My life force, my money, my passion for living, were all getting sucked out of me.

My contract and education from cohabitating with LQ was about to come to an end. I realized that if it didn't, I would come to an end instead. I did a series of intense curse reversal ceremonies inspired and directed by my spirit guide, Hal. These ceremonies were filled with forceful, passionate energies, designed to take my power back and demand transformation.

The most unlikely events transpired after that. New people and opportunities started appearing in my life that supported my transformation. I witnessed a miracle when LQ finally moved out of my house after five freaking years, and then out of my life by the grace of a new client/friend, Amikah. Somehow she broke through the energetic barriers that surrounded me and was able to assist with her financial and energetic resources. She later became my best friend, business, and W.S. partner. I know that without a doubt, Amikah saved my life and for that I am eternally grateful!

I am now "in the flow," something that previously seemed possible only for other people, not me. My spirit guides used to tell me that as hideous as my life was during those dark days of my initiation, the polarity would one day flip, and my life would be as good as it had been bad. They said my life would turn from tragic to magick. I know now what they said was true, as it is already unfolding. I have experienced some of the most wonderful synchronicities recently, which tells me I am precisely in the right place at the right time. I am seeing more 55 or 555's, the code number of my spirit guide, Hal and I know I'm in the zone. I now have a grand education under my belt to assist others, and I am still alive to tell about it.

I beat the odds, and if you are in a similar situation as I was, this should give you inspiration and the hope that you can reverse it too!

Ghosts' Stories

As Ghostbusters, we have come across some memorable ghosts. Sometimes the details of these trapped spirits' lives are so clear, we feel a very close connection with them. The remarkable thing is that we both see different angles of the same story without conversing about it. As an empath, Ronnie goes through their emotional trauma right along with them as the pictures of their stories crystallize. These are just a few of the accounts that have made a lasting impression on us.

It Don't Matter if You're Black or White

Clemson University in South Carolina has its own radio program. It was around Halloween, and the Ghostbuster Gals were asked to do a Halloween show. Sara, the host of the show, was very interested in the paranormal and a believer in ghosts, but the technical support person was not. Neither one of us knew much about the University and had never even seen pictures of it.

While chatting on a three-way call with Sara, Ronnie said she was feeling some strange energy in the top right hand corner of the building Sara was calling from. Sara laughed and told us the area Ronnie had described was where their studio was located. There was also a large antenna on that side of the building.

Not thinking any more about it, Ronnie then reported on another area a bit farther away where she was picking up some very intense vibes. Sara laughed again and said, "Oh, that's the cemetery." No wonder the energy was so dynamic. Cemeteries are one of the most haunted places on the planet. We went on to record the show, but a few days later received this email from Sara:

> Hi Gals,
> The interview went really well. There was only one problem. When we played it back, there was a mysterious swooshing sound, and the volume was nowhere near what we were hearing during the interview! Kinda cool, but unusable for radio, so kinda sad at the same time.
> Is there any way we can do it again? Is it possible?
> Thanks.
> Sara

In talking with Sara, we also found out there were some other weird things that happened in their studio. Bizarre electrical events occurred that they were unable to rationalize away. The final straw was when the printer turned itself on and started spewing papers all over the office. The technical engineer absolutely freaked out, and instantly became a believer since there was no logical explanation for the incidents that had transpired.

Before doing the show for the second time, we decided it would be in everyone's best interest to clear the energy in the studio. We then tuned into some of the buildings and grounds around the campus.

We could sense that there were quite a few ghosts roaming around, so we recorded the program and went about the business of clearing as much as we could.

Using our remote viewing abilities, we investigated an area with large beautiful trees. Even though it looked lush and tranquil, the energy was very dark and depressing. We realized some of these trees had been used for hangings.

One tree in particular had quite a few souls milling about. There was one white man among the "Negroes." Ronnie started to telepathically communicate with him because he seemed so out of place. This is what she gleaned from the "conversation." The man's name was Jon Andersen. In the mid 1800's he came to this country from Sweden with his wife Isabella and young son, Jakob. The Civil War had just ended and he felt he could apply his blacksmithing skills in an area that was rebuilding.

Being of Swedish descent, Jon had no prejudices about his fellow man. Skin color did not matter to him, and he treated everyone with equal respect. This did not go over well with the "good ole boys" of the town, many of which were still slave owners and not adjusting to the new rules.

One day a young black man, Justus Price, who did odd jobs around Jon's shop, was falsely accused of raping the teenage daughter of a wealthy plantation owner. (The details are not clear as to what actually happened with the young girl and whether she was even raped at all, is in question. The reason for the vagueness is because when we tuned into the ghosts, we could only get the information they had from their limited earthly perspective and not from an expanded "birds eye view.")

Jon knew Justus did not perpetrate this heinous crime since he was working with him at the time the alleged rape occurred. So, he stepped forward to defend him. Justus was still thrown in jail and no amount of pleading from Jon made any difference. There were a lot of ugly dynamics going on at the time, and Justus was being railroaded. The mob that had come for him also became very angry with Jon for trying to protect him.

Later that night, six men with white robes, conical hats, and hoods, took Justus from the jail, then broke into Jon's house and grabbed him along with his family. There was terror and confusion in the eyes of his wife and son. They were all thrown in a wagon with Justus, and taken out to, "The Hanging Tree." Waiting nearby were two more men that stood with torches blazing. A noose hung expectantly from the tree.

Leaving Justus in the wagon, they forced the Andersens out. Justus had his hands tied in front of him, and his feet were bound. As some of the men pointed rifles on the Andersen family, another man pulled the wagon up to the tree. Then the rope was placed around Justus' neck. He was so angry that he was dying for something he didn't do, but more importantly he was beside himself that Jon and his family were suffering because of him. The last thing he saw as the wagon was pulled away was the agony on the face of the man who had befriended him.

Now, it was Jon's turn. Six men formed a circle around him. Another restrained his wife, and one held his seven-year-old son. Forcing his family to watch, they beat and kicked him until he could no longer stand. "Nigger lover," they shouted as they continued to pummel him. "This will teach you, you foreign bastard. You don't belong here anyway." Face bloody, body bruised, ribs broken, thinking only of his wife and son, they dragged Jon up on the wagon and positioned the noose around his neck.

Isabel screamed, Jakob sobbed as they deliberately moved the wagon away slowly, leaving Jon struggling to keep a foothold on the bed until the last moment when he no longer had anything solid to hold his weight. The rope tightened instantly but since his neck was not immediately snapped, his instincts were to try and grab it to catch a breath. However, Jon was just too exhausted to loosen the rope enough to breathe. Knowing his family was watching in horror, made his anguish worse. Jon began convulsing as death slowly took him. His last thought was, *"What will happen to my family..."*

After viewing this, we were sickened, and our priorities immediately shifted. We had to help these poor suffering ghosts to the Light and set them free. We immediately opened a portal by the trees and helped not only Jon and Justus, but many others that had been hung in the area. It is interesting to note that Isabella and Jakob were there to escort Jon "home."

Laura Lee's attention kept going back to the unfortunate trees. As she scanned the area, she found that they were devastated by the historical destruction that took place on their limbs. Laura Lee tuned into the trees and this is what they conveyed, "Please...can you help us? This negative energy has been stuck here for many decades, and is not only creating suffering for us, but everything around us as well. We need our freedom again. We need to clear this darkness permanently and we think you are the one that knows how to do it."

Laura Lee immediately put Kryahgenetics Eggs around the trees and started cleaning out the pain, misery and distress that had been inflicted on them. There was some kind of matrix or grid around this area that kept the hideous energy repeating over and over again.

Usually trees can filter and clear energies themselves. That's why some people hug trees, but this situation was different. Somehow the negative vibration got stuck in time, and put this energy on a continuous loop. The trees were surrounded by this heavy, dark, hateful, fearful, force.

Then, an amazing thing happened as Laura Lee removed the matrix. Everything began to get back in sync. The trees started to respond and moved into hyper transformation mode. Soon they were clear, (and it didn't take years and years of therapy to get them stable and functional again). They graciously thanked her, and were now free to hold their branches up with renewed life force and dignity. What a gratifying sight to witness their rejuvenation.

Who are Those Ladies in the Window?

When your four year old little girl is sitting in the car that has just pulled into your driveway and looks up at your living room window and says, "Mommy, why are those two ladies in our house?" and you know there is no one there... Who ya gonna call?

This was the case with one of our clients in California. We had previously removed a female ghost from their home that had already caused two miscarriages. This trapped soul had lost her own baby and once released, our client was able to deliver a healthy daughter.

We received a call about the two female squatters and set out to find out who they were, and why they were there.

After our meditation, we telepathically connected with these women, and here's the tale that was imparted.

It was the late 1800's; Elizabeth and Abigail Henly were sisters. Complications during the birth of the younger sister, Abigail, not only caused the death of their mother, but also left Abigail mentally retarded as well. Elizabeth was about thirteen years older than her baby sister, and the job of mother fell upon her shoulders. Elizabeth grew up to be a schoolteacher and always kept Abigail by her side. Devoted to her challenged sibling, she never married or had children of her own. At the time of their deaths they were forty-five and thirty-two respectively. In the image they projected, they both wore long dresses and had long hair.

One beautiful summer's day as the sisters were eating lunch by the river, Abigail witnessed someone throwing a puppy into the water. She immediately jumped in to save it, with no regard to the fact that she did not know how to swim. Instantly she got into trouble as the river was deep and fast flowing. Elizabeth heard her sister's panicked cry and jumped in to try to rescue her. Abigail flailed about in abject terror, gulping down water as she tried to breathe. Elizabeth was barely able to reach her because the current and the weight of her clothes hindered her progress. Finally, their hands touched for a brief moment and Abigail grabbed on for dear life as she went under. Elizabeth, already exhausted from the struggle to reach her sister, was pulled down by her, and they both drowned. Guilt and fear were so pervasive as they passed, their souls became stuck. Elizabeth became trapped because she wasn't paying attention to Abigail when she went in the water and she felt very guilty that she could not save her. Abigail became a captive because she knew she was responsible for her beloved sister's death.

We wondered why the two sisters came to stay in our clients' living room. Unfortunately their souls were very confused, and the answers were not forthcoming. So many trapped souls have a type of fogginess or amnesia. Knowing the two children that lived in the home were Crystal Kids, we believe these spirits were drawn in by the higher vibration. It is also possible since Elizabeth was a teacher, she was attracted to the young energy as well. After constructing a portal, the Angels came to take these ladies "home."

Laura Lee's Close Encounter With an "Ass Soul"

NOTE: *Here is a little background on why this subtitle is so funny to us. One of my spirit guides, Hal, is noted for his tremendous sense of humor and his ability to play on words. His humor usually has a hidden meaning, and he helps to put things in a perspective that is sometimes bizarre, or "out of this world." Hal has also reminded us quite often when we forget, that laughter can heal most of the things that ail us. One day I heard Hal say, "Yes, there* sure is a real problem with some of those **Ass Souls** you have down there." I just cracked up. It amused me down to my very core. When I told Ronnie, we both laughed so hard we could barely breathe. Something really puzzled us though. We could not believe that **we** didn't come up with this obvious play on words ourselves! As you might have already guessed, Hal has helped inspire some of the humor in this book.

Okay, on with the story.

In the beginning of the year 2000 I met a young man of seventeen years through the Internet. His name was Lother, he lived in Romania, and was born in Transylvania of all places! Lother found the Mistyc House website intriguing and started emailing me. As time went on, we became great Internet buddies and shared a great deal of W.S. information with each other. After extensive communication, I found out some very interesting things about Lother's background and family.

I learned that Lother's father was what they called an "Impresario." That equated to being the manager of a school that taught exotic dancing. It was also a placement service after the young women had completed the school. Many women in repressed Romania could not afford the school, so they literally became slaves until their debt was paid off. They did this by handing over the money they earned to the boss. Numerous improprieties were laced throughout this business, and many women had to pay and pay and pay in order to get released from their contracts. Lother's father's conduct with these women was despicable. He treated them as his personal property because in many ways, he owned them.

Lother told me stories of how his father would sit him down for a "father son talk." In one of these sessions, his father explained the art of knocking someone off without a trace. "You just push them off a cliff. Then if you are investigated weeks or months later, you simply tell the authorities that you don't know where you were on the date in question.

This works because people don't usually remember what they did at a certain time several weeks or months ago." He also stressed that in order to make it big in this world, the best way is through underground businesses like running guns, drugs, and of course selling sex.

Lother had no interest in his father's business and spent most of his free time on the computer doing W.S. research, or playing video games. He also spearheaded the local anime community, which taught him a lot about how to work and interact with people. When Lother's father asked him what he wanted to do with his life, he replied that he aspired to do something to help people. His father just laughed at him as if to say, "how pathetic." Lother related many more stories of how this man had taken advantage of people, especially "his girls," through coercion or blackmail. Lother said that in his country, shysters and gangsters are "the norm," and I concluded that his father was up there at the top of the food chain.

In the spring of 2001, Ronnie and I were working quite closely together. We had rekindled a friendship that went back several years prior. We would walk laps around a nearby park, sometimes with Ronnie's two malamutes leading the way. Ronnie knew of Lother and had even talked to him a few times on the phone.

One evening as we were walking and talking, Lother's name came up in conversation. All of a sudden Ronnie froze, and then exclaimed, "His dad is going to die!" Then she shook her head and said, "Where did **that** come from?" I was surprised too and said, "I don't know, maybe it is a premonition of a heart attack or something?" "All I'm sensing is that he will die in September," she replied. We both thought it was odd because Ronnie didn't usually receive information like this. I decided to tell Lother since he was into W.S. and this certainly qualified. Lother took it in stride and thought his dad would certainly be a candidate for death since his lifestyle and eating habits were conducive for a heart attack. Several weeks went by, not much more was thought about it.

Then, the first day of September I got an email from Lother...his father was dead. He had been murdered!

The real story did not come out until later. Lother's father was shot on the street by a man who was the boyfriend of "one of his girls." Obviously there was so much sleazy corruption and dishonesty going on, the boyfriend was desperate and angry enough to take matters into his own hands.

I was trying to be a good support system for Lother by helping him realize that he was eighteen now and had to grow up and smarten up as well. Then the strangest thing happened over the next few days. His father started coming to my house here in the States! (Usually ghosts hang out in close proximity of where they died. However, there seemed to be some kind of magnetic glitch, and he was able to come across the world and hang out with me!)

At first I wasn't sure what was happening, but got savvy really fast. I was also perplexed as to why of all people he would come to me. I thought he hated me because I was filling his son's head with shameful things like being honorable, conducting himself like a modern day knight, and living by the Knight's Code that I have on my website. I was more than a little annoyed, as he just hung around and grated on my energy. I was especially irritated when he would sit there and watch me exercise. I told him he needed to leave me alone, and go help his family get the estate cleaned up. Finally he left.

Then on the day of his funeral, who shows up...that's right, creepy old Dad! I asked him what the heck he was doing back here, and told him he needed to be with his family to let them know where he left all the important documents he hadn't told anyone about. He said petulantly, "I don't want to." I then replied, "It's time to face the music. You need to tell Lother that you are sorry for all the garbage you taught him." With that, I energetically kicked his behind back to Romania.

A short time later, guess who shows up again? That's right, and now I'm beyond annoyed, I'm ticked off! I shouted, "What are you doing back here! You need to be at your funeral! What don't you get about that!?" He replied, (or rather whined), "I went back and tried to talk to them and no one would listen. They couldn't hear me... It's hard to talk to the living!"

Now part of me was very amused at what I had just heard, and part of me was just plain mad. I then said, "That's not my problem. You figure it out! You made this wrinkled bed, now you sleep in it!" I again kicked his ghostly behind back to Romania and this time energetically held him there until he got his affairs in order.

When everything was completed, I sent that Ass Soul packing through the tunnel along with escorts to make sure he went straight to his life review. I knew he was **not** thrilled about that, but, oh well, he needed to *finally* be responsible for all his underhanded business dealings, the pain and suffering he had put so many women through, and especially what he had done to try to warp his son. It was a pleasure for me to make sure he got where he needed to go.

The interesting thing is, even with the corrupted vile existence this man lived, something wonderful came from his life, and that was his son. This is what Lother told me recently, "My father has served as a constant example of everything I don't want to be, he was the exact opposite of what I feel I am in my core. As such, the resulting contrast actually helped me become who I am today."

Cabin Fever

One Friday evening we had scheduled a ghostbusting for clients near Lake Christina, British Columbia. There were some disturbing things going on in the cabin next to their house and this couple, who we had done some previous work for, were very worried about their young son.

Normally, we always do our ghostbusting as a team, but unfortunately Laura Lee's best friend Amikah passed away that morning, and Laura Lee was in no condition to immerse herself in clearing work. However, since we considered this an emergency situation, it was decided that Ronnie would go ahead and do the busting herself.

Built in 1942, the cabin had some very strange energy attached to it. As Ronnie psychically connected to it, she perceived a male ghost that was trying to hide from her. Well, no ghost is too fast for Ronnie and she was able to establish that his name was Arthur Bradley Hancock. He was a weasely type of character. As his story unfolded, she could feel his grief, shame and embarrassment and realized that Arthur had taken his own life.

Arthur was a loan processor at the bank and was handling the construction loan for the cabin. His wife, Lillian Carlisle Hancock, was the only thing he was proud of and he worshipped her. Born and raised in America, she was an entertainer in her youth. She was still a real looker and very glamorous. Furs, jewelry, fancy clothes were all part of her persona. In order to keep his wife in the lifestyle she was accustomed to, Arthur starting embezzling money.

After compromising himself at the bank, Arthur began to suspect that Lillian was having an affair with the bank manager, Nathan Osborne. Suave, handsome, sophisticated, debonair are words that would depict Nathan. In Arthur's mind, Nathan had it all and he was very jealous of him.

It didn't take long for Arthur's whole life to begin crashing down around him. Nathan was looking at him very suspiciously. *"Maybe he knows I've been stealing money. He'll turn me in for sure. That bastard is trying to steal the only thing I care about, my gorgeous Lillian. He wants me out of the way so they can be together. I'm ruined."* These are the thoughts that went through Arthur's head as he formulated a plan.

Early one evening, after the construction crew had gone for the day, Arthur lured Nathan out to the cabin under false pretenses. The roof and the exterior had not been completed as of yet, although it was framed in. As they walked into the back room, Arthur confronted Nathan about the affair. Nathan did not deny it. He claimed to love Lillian and wanted her for his own. Nathan then confronted Arthur about the money shortages and said he was ready to go to the authorities about it.

Arthur was devastated. His two greatest fears were now a reality. There was nothing left of his life. Anger and rage consumed him as he pulled out a small revolver from his pocket. He then proceeded to shoot Nathan in the chest four times.

Looking around the construction site in desperation, Arthur was able to find some rope and a large barrel that he moved into position. He then climbed up on the barrel and secured the rope on an exposed rafter. Crying and sniveling, he tied the rope around his neck. While looking at Nathan's dead body, thinking of how Lillian had betrayed him, Arthur Bradley Hancock stepped off his perch to his death.

Unfortunately, hanging can leave quite a messy corpse. As Ronnie looked a little closer at the tortured soul of Arthur Hancock, she could see that his eyes were bulging, his tongue was swollen, and his pants were soiled. He also gave off an obnoxious odor (probably from the stinking pants). When she quizzed the owners of the cabin, they verified that the room in question did indeed smell bad at times.

The two ghosts remained trapped in the back room of the cabin for years. Then one day a young Crystal boy of five came to stay in the cabin. While in that room, Nathan convinced Arthur to suck the boy's energy in order to weaken him. The boy then became ill with a high fever. His parents could find no reason for their son to be burning up.

The boy's auric field was sufficiently deteriorated that Nathan was able to shove in to his being.

This little boy's personality changed dramatically and not for the better. Nathan was a very high-powered, controlling, authoritative being who was used to getting his own way. Along with a high level of intelligence, he was very manipulative as well. So, this sweet little boy was now being controlled by a powerful entity that enjoyed making everyone around him miserable. This was one of the main reasons his parents had called us.

As Ronnie worked to remove Nathan from the child's field, she was met with a lot of resistance. Nathan liked his new "home" and enjoyed his newfound freedom.

Ronnie put a Kryahgenetics Egg around him and Nathan started to become belligerent, throwing his shoulder into the Egg to try to escape. But try as he would, there was nothing he could do. Nathan just hated being out of control.

Ronnie opened a portal and was surprised when Lillian came for him. He must have been surprised as well when he asked, "Lillian is it really you?" All of a sudden his demeanor softened, and joy filled his spirit. As Nathan started up the portal with the love of his life, he turned back to the boy and said, "Thanks for the ride, kid."

Turning her attention back to Arthur, he had become very agitated. Pacing around the room he shouted, "I am not going anywhere!" Ronnie could sense that he was afraid he would be going to Hell. "I am not going. I am not going!" Trying to calm Arthur down, Ronnie psychically projected herself into the room and sat on the bed. She asked Arthur to join her. When he did, he whispered to her..."There's somebody else here, you know."

As Ronnie checked around, she sensed a female presence. Arthur said, "It's a Lady of the Night." Ronnie thanked him for alerting her to the ghost that was hiding in another room. As the Angels began to assist in opening a portal, Ronnie wracked her brain to see who she could call to escort Arthur "home." She wondered if Lillian might also come for him. However, waiting in the tunnel was Arthur's mother, Anna. The two of them always had a special connection. As Arthur moved into the portal to join his mother, his appearance transformed from grotesque and smelly to youthful and clean. He actually thanked Ronnie as he was released from his hell and headed "home."

Searching for the female entity, Ronnie indeed found a "Lady of the Night" who was murdered by a religious fanatic. Her name was Mae Jean. Young and desperate, she had turned to prostitution for survival.

Mae Jean began to enjoy the lifestyle her profession afforded her and was never lacking for customers. In this small but thriving town, there was a young man who was brought up in a very strict Christian household. This man was very conflicted as he was attracted and repulsed by Mae Jean at the same time.

Consumed by his own demons, late one night, this disturbed young man dragged Mae Jean behind a building, threw her to the ground, and screamed in her face about how evil she was. Ranting and raving, he was practically foaming at the mouth with rage. Then, while staring in her eyes, he choked the life out of her.

Ronnie actually felt sorry for Mae Jean. That trapped ghost truly believed she was evil and deserved to die. These are the thoughts that trapped her in the first place. Jeshua (Jesus) Himself came to assist in this soul's rescue. As He stood at the portal entrance, Jeshua said to Mae Jean, "Your time here is done. It is time to come home. The Father awaits." He held out His hand to her and with some encouragement from Ronnie, Mae Jean was set free from her earthly bonds. Jeshua thanked Ronnie for her service and Ronnie thanked Him for His assistance.

Here is a letter from our client, sharing his perceptions.

We had been having problems (W.S.) at our current home. A friend of ours had been helping us clear our house. When it became apparent that the problems were not going away, they found The Ghostbuster Gals for us.

Ronnie and Laura Lee immediately gave our house a calm feeling after they found and cleared up significant problems. As we dug deeper, we found that our vacation cabin also held a lot of history. It was polluted with problems... our children (who are very bright Crystal children) were easy targets for these outside energies to attach to. It took us almost two years of trying to figure out what was going on, and how to get a handle on things.

Our cottage was on land next to an old nightclub...lots of dark history. We found that a Shove-In had gotten into our little boy and was altering his behaviour. He was a nasty man. He first entered our boy when he was sleeping. Our son woke screaming and hallucinating, and ran a very high temperature for over a day. Ronnie cleared our son of this and many other things, told us of history of the land, and even removed smells that were present in the cabin.

Ronnie and Laura Lee were able to remove negative energy vortexes that broke every new item we brought into our house...nothing new ever worked...until now.

My wife and I often wonder what we would have done if we had not heard of The Ghostbuster Gals. They have given our home a sense of calmness again and our children are back to being themselves. We wonder how many other parents might be going through something similar.

What we did...be open-minded and reach out for help... is only a call away.

B.

Do You Know Where Your Departed Loved Ones Are?

One of the purposes of this chapter as with the entire book is to help alleviate the fear of death. There is so much of it in the world. When people start to understand that death is merely a transition from one plane to another, and their consciousness remains intact, they can let go of their fear of death and begin enjoying life.

Where's My Daddy?

Every once in a while a client will ask Ronnie to check on a loved one to see how they are doing. This was the case with a young woman that had come for a reading. As Ronnie telepathically connected with the client's father, she could see that he had not crossed over and was still stuck the house where he had died.

Distraught, the man was pacing back and forth looking for his wife who had made her transition a few months earlier. Apparently when he passed, he was filled with the heavy emotions of guilt, sorrow and anger. He was also in a great deal of pain. This is a recipe for getting caught between the worlds.

Ronnie's client asked if she could help her father cross over. When Ronnie tried to communicate with him, he was foggy-headed and confused as many ghosts are.

Since this was a simple spirit rescue, Ronnie decided to go it alone. Normally, she and Laura Lee work as a team.

Creating a portal in the man's living room, Ronnie asked his wife to come and escort him across. Her client was very relieved that her father was now reunited with her mother. She realized if she had not asked Ronnie to check on her father, he might have been doomed to roam his home alone.

Messages From Beyond the Veil

Occasionally while praying before a private reading, Ronnie will feel the presence of a spirit with whom she is not familiar. Sometimes it's very subtle and sometimes it knocks her over the head. Recently, this was the case when she was preparing for a phone reading.

It was a referral client, a friend of a friend of another client. As she was preparing, a very strong female presence was in her face. Ronnie asked who she was, and received the name Margaret.

The first thing Ronnie asked when her client called was, "Do you know anyone named Margaret?" The woman thought and thought and then said she knew a Marguerite.

Figuring that was close enough, Ronnie went about giving the messages from the spirit contact. Even though her client couldn't quite figure out why Marguerite would contact her, she was pleased with the information.

About two weeks later, Ronnie was at a Dannion Brinkley workshop that she had organized, and the same client came up to her apologizing profusely. She said she had remembered a very close friend that had died a number of years ago, named Margaret, and now she has a lot more clarity from the messages. Ronnie chuckled to herself because it is common for people to get a type of amnesia when it comes to dealing with the dead. (Just ask James Van Praagh, world famous medium.)

Ronnie's Gift

Three weeks after their sixteen-year-old son had been shot in the back, the parents came over from Seattle to see me. Their grief was palpable. I told them I couldn't promise contact with their son James, but I would try.

Maybe it was because James was newly dead, or maybe it was because he was such a bright soul, but he came through to me clearer than any of my previous contacts with the deceased. He had crossed over quickly even though he died in such a violent way. That was a tremendous relief to his parents.

James showed me a picture of his room with lots of trophies in it. He still had an attachment to them, and was worried about what would happen to these prized possessions. I mentioned this to his parents who confirmed that, yes indeed, he had a great deal of sports trophies, however, they had boxed them up and put them in the garage.

This agitated James, he wanted to make sure I told his parents not to get rid of them. He also showed me a flannel shirt that was in his closet. I described it to his parents who looked at each other in amazement. That was his favorite shirt, and he wore it whenever he could. James asked them not to get rid of that either.

One of the reasons I think James was so specific with the things he showed me was so his father, who sat very quietly through the whole reading, would not have any doubts that it was indeed his son.

Then James gave me the most incredible gift I have ever received from someone who had passed into the next realm.

He showed me what his mother looked like through his eyes. It was mind boggling to say the least. She was absolutely radiant, and her energy field stretched up through the house into the sky. It was filled with pastel colors that were sparkling and pulsating. James explained that each of us has a similar field with its own unique energy signature.

It answered a lot of questions for me as I sometimes wondered what we looked like to our unseen friends. And I hate to admit as silly as it sounds, I wondered about them seeing us in the bathroom, making love or any other personal situations. Now I understood that they don't actually see us in our human form, but as this brilliantly beautiful, glowing field of light. How illuminating!

Since that time I have done numerous readings for James' mother and sister. Sometimes he comes through to offer comfort and support, and sometimes to give them a gentle kick in the butt. The one common thread is that James reminds them that he is always there, loving them with all his heart and soul.

This is a letter from James' mother sharing her experience of the reading.

> *Three weeks after my son died, I contacted Ronnie for a reading. I had never had a reading before but someone sent me a card and said, "This is my gift to you." It had Ronnie's name and phone number on it.*
>
> *I called Ronnie and set up an appointment to see her a week later. When I arrived at Ronnie's house and we went down stairs to her room, the lights were flickering on and off and Ronnie told us that James had been with her all afternoon and was very excited that we had come.*
>
> *As Ronnie started the reading, she asked if she could give it to us just the way James talked, because he was talking very fast. James started talking about his*

trophies. He was worried about what we were going to do with them.

While my husband Jim and I were driving to Ronnie's from Seattle, we had spoken about our son's trophies and wondered what we should do with all of them. Well, we received our answer, because James quite emphatically asked us to keep them, as they kept us connected. He was very proud of his trophies.

He also mentioned his favorite shirt and said, "Keep what is important, Mom, especially my shirt, and give the rest away."

As Ronnie continued, James said, "Mom, your light is so bright." He was telling Ronnie he was in awe of what he saw when he looked at me. Then he gave Ronnie a vision so she could see what he was seeing.

James then spoke of his older sister and how they were soul family, and she was a mother figure to him. He spoke of his middle sister who is disabled, and he said she was not soul family but he had great compassion for her.

James spoke to his father, Jim, and told him about another lifetime where they had been twin brothers. In that lifetime Jim had stepped in front of a horse to save James' life, and Jim ended up dying from a head injury. This made total sense to both my husband and myself, because for years, Jim had unexplainable headaches in the back of his head. Once Ronnie shared James' words, Jim stopped having the headaches!

James also told his dad that in that lifetime he had never gotten over the death of his twin brother and he asked his father not to continue that pattern now that he was the one that was gone.

It was an incredible reading, which helped Jim and I understand that James was still very much with us, and that he was aware of our grief in losing him. He let us know that he was sending us comforting energy.

Over the last ten years, we have had many visits from James. He seems very connected to Ronnie and comes to give messages for us to help us move forward in our journey. John Edwards, a famous medium, has said that James is the strongest in spirit that he has encountered. He didn't just give symbols, but spoke directly to you.

Ronnie has been an incredible inspiration to my family and I know that James loves her as we do.

Nancy Wolf

When You Least Expect It

Many years ago, Ronnie belonged to a healing group that met every Thursday evening. On one of those nights there was a new woman named Linda who attended the meeting.

Here is Ronnie's account of what happened that night:

As we were all standing around a young man on the massage table, I looked over at Linda and saw she was fidgeting and shrugging her shoulders as if in pain. I then asked Linda for permission to tune into what was going on. After I received an affirmative, I shared what I was picking up.

"You have an older woman that is very fearful, stuck in your energy field. It feels like she was very religious and is afraid she is going to Hell." I continued my description, "She speaks with a heavy accent and doesn't know much English. Do you know who she is?" Linda, with a shocked look on her face replied, "That's my mother! She died a few months ago, and I was there with her. She was born and raised in Italy and almost never spoke English."

Well, Linda's mother was stuck in her auric field. She was not only weighing Linda down, but sucking her energy as well. I could see her mother over her left shoulder, and that was where her pain was located.

It is not uncommon for people who are fearful when they pass, to jump into the field of someone familiar to them. It can temporarily bring them comfort and perceived safety. The problem is since the electromagnetic fields are incompatible it can cause a tremendous drain on the "host." The ghosts don't get to cross over and experience a life review or continue on their evolutionary path. They are just stuck and become stagnant and unfulfilled.

I asked Linda if she would like me to help her mother go to the Light. She said she would be most grateful if I would do that. As I opened a portal, her mother buried her head further into her daughter's field. She was so afraid to look she was actually trembling. I then asked Jesus to please come and help with this lost soul. Feeling the energy of Christ, Linda's mother pulled her head out to take a peek. Overcome with emotion, she dropped to her knees and wept. Jesus took her by the hand and took her "home." Linda exclaimed that she felt so much lighter after her mother was gone, and the pain vanished as well.

You Can't Always Get What You Want

Ronnie did a reading for two sisters that were clients of hers. Normally they had separate readings, but since their mother had passed away recently, they were hoping for a message from her.

Instead of their gentle sweet mother, Ronnie started receiving information from a very strong male presence. A thick accent was pervasive in the transmission. (Her clients are from the Middle East.) She could sense that this was a relative and his name had a J sound associated with it. When Ronnie mentioned this to the sisters they immediately said, "Oh no. Not Uncle George! We don't want to talk to him." Well, of course it was Uncle George and he had plenty he wanted to say to them, starting with an apology.

These women were so hurt by their uncle's actions, they could not find it in their hearts to forgive him, even though Ronnie suggested they find a way to do it for their own sakes. In fact one of the sisters actually started yelling at him. Uncle George tried to explain why he did the things he did and that he only had their best interest at heart, but they would have none of it. There was too much water under the bridge and too much pain they were still carrying for it to have any affect.

Ronnie could see that this soul was suffering for his choices and that he wanted to be forgiven so he could move on, but the sisters adamantly refused to do anything they perceived would help him. There was nothing more she could do and had to chalk it up to Karma.

Breaking Up is Hard to Do

There is a dynamic that takes place when people are clingy and co-dependent on a deceased person, refusing to let them go. Without realizing it, they can literally turn that person into a ghost! It is our experience that after people die in a supportive, loving environment, they immediately cross over and may get some kind of debriefing before they go for their life review. This brings clarity about "the bigger picture."

When souls are able to go to the Light, they are free to come back to this reality temporarily and support the ones left behind during their time of grief and loss. They can stay for several days to several months, and then may move on to another assignments or adventures on the "other side."

Many, many different avenues and directions are available for souls at this point in their evolution. One of those possibilities is for the deceased person to go to what we call "Guide School," and become a spirit guide for loved ones that are here on Earth. We are seeing this happen more often within the past several years, and it seems to be picking up as time passes. It appears that when the frequencies of the Earth elevate, it places more challenges and demands on our physical bodies, so we can use all the help we can get. Who better to support us than someone who has lived here and knows what those challenges are...someone who knows us and loves us!

Guide School is a wonderful program, and it assists everyone involved. The guide gets to be in service and interact with former friends and family, while receiving a great spirit education along the way. The people still in bodies receive the grace of having someone they can really connect with, support them in their Earth challenges. It's a win-win situation.

There is however a huge glitch in the system when humans get wrapped up in their own grief, pain, and especially guilt over a loved one who has passed. The guilt is the worst part, and can get twisted and warped. In turn it warps and twists the entire energetics, which can create all sorts of problems. It may cause the loved one to remain around the earth plane and not move on, thus becoming a ghost.

We have seen situations where after someone passes away, the individuals left behind get so out of balance they almost worship the person who is no longer present. They may even make a shrine in their home to the dearly departed. They feel obligated to hold on to everything connected to their loved one; clothes, cars, jewelry, knickknacks, dishes, animals, etc.

Now, we are not saying it's a bad thing to enjoy the items you have inherited from a loved one. That's fine. The problems begin when you have extreme feelings of guilt and disloyalty for getting rid of deceased loved one's possessions.

This can be very detrimental to both parties and creates a mental instability inspired by guilt, shame and fear. This energy is destructive to everyone. It may cause the loved one to remain around the earth plane and not move on, thus becoming a ghost.

A deceased uncle of a friend of Laura Lee's appeared to her to see if she could contact his wife. He wanted to make sure that his wife got rid of his stuff because he sure didn't need it anymore. The energy surrounding it was holding both of them back. The uncle told her that his wife needs the space for new business projects, and his stuff is just in her way.

Laura Lee thought it was odd that the uncle chose to come to her, a perfect stranger to both he and his wife, but she assumed that it was the only way he could get that message through to his beloved. Laura Lee relayed this information to her friend, who in turn forwarded this to his aunt.

The aunt was a bit taken aback by it all, but listened, and tried to understand. It took her about nine months, plus an additional message from another psychic for her to really acknowledge this challenge. Once she had decided to heed this advice and get rid of her husband's stuff, her business, which they had jointly run, started picking up. She could then see she had been damming herself all this time. Now she realizes what was told to her by Laura Lee a year ago was correct. When she tried to hold on to her husband by holding on to his things, the energy got stuck and out of balance. This caused a chain reaction that spiraled down to everything in her life, putting the business in jeopardy. Fortunately, she was able to correct the situation freeing not only herself, but her husband as well.

We understand how hard it is to lose a loved one. We have had our share of loss and have experienced the range of emotions that go along with it. Through our own knowledge, and especially with Ronnie's expertise in assisting people in her hospice volunteer work with The Twilight Brigade/Compassion in Action, we understand the dynamics of dying and how to make sure that both sides get what they need.

We live in a society that exploits the vulnerability that death can create. The industry of death has pulled in millions and millions of dollars spent on caskets and grave plots for people who are dead. The dead don't really care whether or not the box they are buried in is plush inside or plain, or if the grave is next to a beautiful tree or not. They really don't care or need huge sprays of flowers put on the box. The flowers will wilt and die. One or two flowers to bring fragrance and stability to those that are here are just as good as dozens. Many times, a funeral can put a huge financial hardship on the loved ones left behind since they now have the added burden of paying the bills.

In many ways it is the corporate/consumer attitude of having to keep up with the Joneses that has turned death into a huge industry. It is also to the advantage of the funeral home to convince you that your loved one deserves the ultra fancy casket with the beautiful satin lining, and the peaceful setting in the cemetery, as this is their livelihood! It is outrageous how much money is spent **"over our dead bodies."** It is almost bordering on decadence.

If you are wondering whether you have fallen into one of these traps, ask yourself: "Am I obsessive about the death of a loved one? Am I spending more money than necessary for funeral expenses? Are my thoughts and feelings about my deceased loved one keeping me from living? Am I holding on to things that are useless to me? Am I holding onto things that I could give to someone who would actually use them? Am I holding onto stuff out of guilt, feeling that I am being disloyal and disrespectful if I get rid of it?"

If your answer to any of these questions is "yes," then you may choose to re-evaluate your actions, and take a different approach to your life... and your life without your loved one.

You never really get *over* the loss of someone you love, but you can eventually learn to get through it. We have seen people try to repress their emotions because it's just too painful, and it's easier to practice avoidance and denial. Ultimately, these emotions, if not honored can come back to haunt us.

One of the lessons that Ronnie teaches in her hospice workshops is on grief and bereavement. It is important to understand that there is no timetable for the mourning process. However to move into the healing process the acronym T.E.A.R. can be very beneficial: **T**o accept the loss. **E**xperience the grief. **A**djust to the loss. **R**einvest in the new reality.

When this formula is followed, it decreases the chances of a loved one remaining around the earth plane without moving on, thus becoming a ghost.

Pets are Departed Loved Ones Too...

Puppy's Passing Produces Epiphany for Laura Lee

Puppy, (what an original name for a dog, eh?) was a wonderful Sheltie mix who was a part of our family for over seventeen years. In fact, she was in the family almost three years longer than any of my kids! She could sing and dance and performed many times in small venues. Her favorite song to sing with was "Ghost Riders In the Sky." Puppy really got into it, especially during the chorus, "Yi-pi-yi-aaaaay...Yi-pi-yi-ooooo...ghost riders in the sky." She would throw back her head and howl 'til she was out of breath.

People just loved Puppy, since she had some very wonderful qualities. She thought that everyone knew her name because most of the time when strangers would see her they'd say, "Ooh, look at the cute puppy."

Puppy was good with the kids, but after my fourth baby was born, she had grown a little weary. She would put her paws on the cradle and look in, then look at me and my husband, then look back at the baby, then look at us again as if to say, "You have **got** to be kidding, **not another one!**" Then she walked slowly out of the room with an attitude of, "Don't get me involved, it's not my job."

Puppy had been a mother to several litters herself. She delivered her second one, which was conceived when she ran off with a pack of neighborhood dogs, about two months before I had my first son Reuben. So, we went through a pregnancy together. I learned how to breathe and stay in control by watching Puppy have puppies. I learned more from observing her than I did in any of the childbirth classes I took!

One hot summer night a few weeks before Reuben was born, I got up to go to the bathroom, and to my surprise, the father of the puppies had come to visit. Between the two of them, they somehow managed to get the wooden screen door opened and they were both sitting in the moonlight together watching the puppies sleep in the box. I couldn't believe what I was seeing and called my husband in to witness this extraordinary sight. It seemed to be a real life version of Lady and the Tramp!

There were three more litters after this. However, the last one almost killed Puppy, and she had to have an emergency C-section. Apparently one of the puppies was blocking the birth canal, and she was fading fast. It was a miracle Puppy pulled through. She had to have her "puppy factory" removed after that. We had been meaning to get her spayed but never seemed to be able to catch her in between pregnancies.

Puppy was such a part of the family, it seemed like she had always been there. She was a trooper through all of the eighteen moves we had made, several which were across the country. One time my husband put a small rug on the tank of his motorcycle for comfort and traction to transport

Puppy to the new house we were building. The car was in the shop and there was no other way to get her there. Part of the trek was a twenty-minute commute on the freeway. People honked and waved and gave them the thumbs up, as it was quite a sight to see. Puppy was a little nervous at first but stayed perfectly still and balanced. She loved having the wind in her face. It was a dog's heaven.

Yes, Puppy was quite a dog, and she had many adventures when we lived in "Mistycah's Mini Mansion." She got the creeps just like we did when things were amiss in the house, and stayed away from the half-baked bathroom behind the laundry room.

Even though Puppy was an extraordinary dog, she would sometimes do things that caused her grief later on. One day she got into my closet and found a three-pound plastic bag full of chocolate chips that I put there to hide from the kids. She must have thought she had died and gone to heaven!

After eating nearly a third of the chocolate chips, Puppy must have thought she had died and gone to hell. She began acting really sick and when I saw the bag of chocolate chips ripped open, I knew why. Puppy threw up most of it and I gave her herbs to clear her system. (She was raised on people food and herbs, and responded very well to natural remedies.) It took about two days, but Puppy somehow pulled through. At the time, I had no idea how lethal chocolate can be for dogs.

In the fall, one of the neighborhood cats got pregnant, and guess where she chose to have her kittens. That's right, in our house on one of the kid's beds! Things were okay as long as Puppy stayed out of the room...that was no problem for her. Then one day my husband decided to take some of the kittens into the master bedroom where Puppy slept. She seemed to like the little kittens and her maternal instincts kicked in. She would sniff at them, then lie down and look at them with her head cocked in fascination. Soon the mother cat came in looking for her kittens and freaked out on

Puppy. Puppy was traumatized. She ran under the bed and stayed there all night.

Now, I don't know what possessed him, but a few days later my husband took another one of the kittens in to see Puppy. She was really leery, but once again the maternal instincts kicked in and she lay down by the kitty and watched it. Well, by this time, mother cat knew exactly where to look. She came charging in and there was another scrap in the bedroom. From that day on, Puppy would not leave the room without a bodyguard and she stayed under the bed most of the time.

Puppy's health started going downhill rapidly after this. It was also a time of transition for all of us. The mansion was put up for sale by the landlady and sold quickly. We had to find another house, which wasn't easy. No one wanted to rent to someone who had four kids and a dog. We finally did find a place, but it had to be cleaned thoroughly since the previous tenants had cats. The carpets were ruined, and it was really hard to get the odor out of the basement.

The scent of cat everywhere seemed to be the last straw for Puppy, and her health started failing. She would do strange things like go to her water bowl and then stop abruptly and walk away. It was like she was checking herself out of life. We would try to hand feed and water her, but that didn't work very well.

A few days later, no one had seen Puppy for a while. It was dark, cold, and a rainstorm was raging. I went looking for her in the house and she wasn't there. I finally found her in the back yard lying under the swing set…it was evident that she went there to die. I scooped her up, brought her into the house and dried her off with towels. I cried and cried, as I realized how serious this was. Sitting there, holding her on my lap, I knew we had to make a decision on what to do with this beloved pet that had been such an important part of the family history. I made an appointment with the vet the next day and told the kids what was happening.

It was a late spring morning in 1994 when my husband, middle son Micah and I took Puppy to the vet. We were all hoping that perhaps there might be something they could do for her. When we arrived we had to wait for a while in the waiting room. Puppy perked up some when a little puppy who was also waiting for an appointment, wanted to play with her. I thought this was a good sign.

When it was our turn, we went in and the vet did some quick tests. The diagnosis wasn't good. She had kidney failure and was severely dehydrated. The vet said there was not much of a chance of fixing it and she was probably in a lot of discomfort. The kindest thing would be to put her down.

This was the hardest decision I ever had to make, but gave them the go ahead and signed the euthanasia papers. They suggested that we leave since sometimes the animals go into convulsions and it would be better if we were not there to witness that.

With tears in my eyes, I gave Puppy one last scratch behind her ears and picked up her muzzle and looked deep into her eyes. I said in my head, "I'm sorry, I'm sooo sooo sorry..." Puppy looked back and the telecommunication we had was quite clear. Puppy replied, "It's okay, don't worry, I understand and it's okay, everything is okay."

This was too much for me and I walked out of the room, ran to the car and burst into tears. We drove home in near silence and when we got there, I ran to my bedroom and shut the door. I waited in numbness till the vet called to tell us that Puppy had been put down and she did not struggle. That helped, but the reality was harsh.

I took it the hardest of anyone in the family. It was a difficult time for me, as I had just been the driving force behind my family leaving organized religion and finding a new spiritual path. Family and friends were furious and we had people calling and writing every day telling us we were going to Hell. I thought that I understood what my position was, but at this point in time, I wasn't quite sure *what* I believed in any more. I was unsure about what happened after this life, and I especially had no idea what might be in store for pets after they died.

For the rest of the day, I stayed holed up in my room and only came out to do what was absolutely necessary. I questioned everything I believed in and eventually wiped the board clean and came to the conclusion I didn't believe in anything and needed to start fresh. The only thing I was sure of was that I loved my kids, and I loved my dog that was no longer with us.

That night as I tried to get some rest, I heard scratching under the bed like Puppy used to do when she was dreaming and her paws would scratch the wood. I also heard the muffled barking that Puppy used to do when she was dreaming. At first this didn't faze me, as it was a normal sound that I had heard for years. Then in my half sleep state, it dawned on me, Puppy was not under the bed, she was dead!

I got up and looked underneath to see if one of the kids had crawled under there, but it was empty...nothing visible anyway. This went on for days. Sometimes I would hear Puppy walking around the house at night, and my questioning brought more clarity. I then opened up and began to get some clear communication with Puppy.

Puppy told me that she was fine and that she was with her "soul mate" and was happy. I didn't know dogs had soul mates. She also said that she would incarnate back into another dog when I was ready and that I would know it was her. This gave me great comfort.

After that I never heard the scratching or barking again. It was now confirmed for me there was indeed an afterlife for animals, that they have similar contracts as we do here, and they evolve spiritually just like humans. After this revelation I stopped mourning and got back to living.

This experience has helped me to assist other pet owners that have had similar losses, to find peace and comfort knowing that an animal's spirit is eternal too.

Ronnie's Tale of Two Kitties

When my faithful cat friend Skylar had to be put to sleep because of an illness, I was devastated. He had been a playmate and companion for over fifteen years.

Skylar moved with me ten different times, in three different states; from Arizona, to Florida and then to Washington. When we finally got to Spokane, things settled down a bit.
After renting for a year, we were able to buy a home. It needed a lot of work and then we were finally ready to move in. We were only there for a couple of days and Skylar was barely starting to get used to it. The new carpet had already been put down, and the walls were freshly painted. The only thing not finished was the overhang by the front door. The work crew started early in the morning tearing it apart, and by early evening everything was back together again.

Around ten o'clock that night, I noticed that Skylar was not in his usual place...by my side on the couch. I looked around the house, in the basement, then called for him outside. He was nowhere to be found. Since we had only been in the house for two days, I was a little nervous since Skylar wasn't familiar with the area.

Starting to get worried, I checked outside again. I strained my ears to pick up any sound. Very faintly, I heard a meow. *"Okay, where's that coming from?"* I thought. Grabbing a flashlight, I looked up into the neighbor's tree, but no Skylar. Then I heard it again, a muffled meow. It was coming from *inside* the roof! Oh my God, Skylar was walled up in the overhang! He must have crawled in while the workers were at lunch and got so scared when they came back he stayed there. I was practically hysterical as I ran inside and called out to my husband Bill, "We have to tear the roof off the new overhang. Skylar is trapped inside!" I was ready to do that with my bare hands to save my Skylar.

My husband, staying calm quickly opened the access to the attic in the hallway ceiling. Climbing up on the stepladder Bill shined a flashlight into the dark recesses. There, staring back were two eyes as big as saucers. It wasn't hard to coax Skylar out of the attic, however, when Bill handed him down to me, he was covered from head to toe with "blown-in" insulation. Desperate times call for desperate measures, as I quickly took him to the kitchen sink. He was not a happy cat as I spray washed the gray powdery stuff off of him. This was only the second time in his ten years of life that he had a bath. For those of you who have bathed a cat before, I think you know what I was up against. For those of you who haven't, suffice it to say, it was not a pretty picture. After I towel dried Skylar, he walked off indignantly.

The very next afternoon, I couldn't find Skylar again. I went around the house inside and out, calling his name. Back in the living room, I thought I heard a faint meow. Again, I wondered, *"Where the heck is that coming from?"* Then I heard it once more. It was coming from the fireplace! Oh my God, this time Skylar had gotten on the roof and fallen into the chimney! He was about at the half way mark, spread eagle, trying to maintain a hold to keep himself from plunging down into the fireplace itself. Yelling for my husband, I panicked, *"What are we going to do?"*

My anxiety increased when we realized it was possible for Skylar to fall down into the basement fireplace, which had an insert. Running down to examine it I wondered, *"How would we ever get him out of there?"*

My pulse was racing as I ran back up to the living room. I tried to look up the chimney to get a peek at how he was doing. All of a sudden, I heard a pitiful cry as Skylar fell the rest of the way down the chimney and plopped into the very dirty fireplace in front of me. I was so relieved he hadn't fallen all the way to the basement, and landed on the insert.

I don't know how we would have rescued him if that happened.

My relief was short lived, however, as Skylar took two sooty steps onto my brand new beige carpet. I watched in horror as he shook himself off, spreading black soot everywhere. I grabbed him up before he could leave any more marks, and guess where he went...right to the kitchen sink... again!

Skylar was now covered from head to toe in soot. What a mess! This time the bath went a little easier. I guess he was getting used to it after the insulation incident. I felt so sorry for my poor kitty. I knew if he wasn't traumatized by the attic adversity, he certainly was now after the fireplace fiasco. Following these two back-to-back calamities, Skylar spent most of the rest of his life safely indoors.

The last relocation Skylar had to make was when I moved into my sister's house after she made her transition "home." He seemed quite content there. A few years later, he became ill and I had to call the vet to come. It was a snowy January afternoon. Skylar was fifteen now and the vet suggested it was time. He put Skylar to sleep in my arms and I cried like a baby. Life was very difficult without Skylar, as he had been my constant companion through all of my moves, my divorce and my sister's passing.

On the one-year anniversary of his death, he paid me a most welcomed visit. It was the middle of the night and I was fast asleep. All of a sudden I felt Skylar walking on the bed and stepping on my body. I wondered if I was dreaming, but I could actually feel him pressing against me as he lay down by my side. I could even hear him purring! I was elated that he had come back, and fell asleep with him curled up next to me. When I awoke the next morning, Skylar was gone.

The second night was even weirder. I could feel his presence nearby but had to reach into his dimension and pull him through to be with me. The surroundings were dark and there were other cats milling about. I had never experienced anything like this before, but it was so vivid and clear.

Again, I questioned whether I was dreaming, but there Skylar was, by my side, soft, warm and furry. I don't remember how long he was there, but I enjoyed every minute of it. He was able to communicate that he was doing fine which brought me great comfort. I hoped for a return visit, but that was the last time I was able to physically experience Skylar.

I still grieved for my buddy and it took me a couple of years to feel I could even bring another cat into my life. About a year and a half later, my son and I moved out to the woods. One bleak January Friday, I decided I was ready to bring a new little kitty into our home. I called the Humane Society and our local animal rescue group, but there were no kittens to be found.

Finally, I called a pet shop and they said they had one male kitten available. He was white with a dark gray spot on his head. I drove into town to check the little guy out. Of course I immediately fell in love with him and took him home to meet my sixteen-year-old son, Josh, who had the same reaction. Josh was into Japanese Anime at the time, and asked if we could call the new member of our family, Rioki. Not being able to deny my only child much of anything, I acquiesced.

Rioki seemed to adjust to his new environment easily, but I noticed he started to lose his appetite within a day or so. He also seemed to tire easily and just wasn't very peppy. Not wanting to take any chances I made an appointment with the vet that Monday. They kept him for a couple of days to run tests. When I went to pick him up, the diagnosis was not definitive. The vet gave me a bottle of Interferon to try. To my delight, it seemed to work and this beautiful kitty grew stronger each day.

Three weeks later the bottle of medicine ran out and little by little Rioki grew weaker and weaker. The last Sunday night we spent together, he crawled under the covers and just hugged my body. Monday, it was back to the vet. She didn't hold much hope but said she would do what she could. I didn't want to leave him, but I had no choice. She called late in the afternoon to say there was nothing more she could do, and she would have to put him down sometime that evening. I was sick to my stomach. I had gotten so attached to this cuddly little ball of fur.

That night as I was preparing to do a radio program with Laura Lee, I was sitting at my computer when I heard Rioki mewing. It was as clear as a bell. A feeling of gratitude emanated from the same direction as the sound. Before I had a chance to process this, Josh walked into the room with a funny look on his face and said, "Mom, the weirdest thing just happened. I swear I heard Rioki in my room." Suddenly, the phone rang. It was the vet calling to let me know she had just put Rioki to sleep a few minutes ago. It was comforting to know that even though Rioki was with us for such a short time, he came to say goodbye before his spirit left this world.

Dead Dog Teaches Ronnie a New Trick

The daughter of a client was coming to Spokane from Montana. She was a Naturopathic Doctor and wanted a reading. When she arrived, she appeared to be a little closed off and unsure of this type of thing. I think her mother might have talked her into it.

We chatted a bit, then I asked her if she had any questions. The doctor responded with, "How's my dog Bailey doing?" Since she was away from home, it seemed like she wanted me to make sure her pet was okay. As I tuned in, I was a little disconcerted and said to her, "Well, maybe Bailey is sleeping right now, because he is presenting himself as not having a physical body. I see him free and cavorting around...Maybe, he's dreaming," I mused.

Nonchalantly she replied, "Oh, Bailey is dead. He died a few months ago. I just wanted you to check on him and see how he is." I started to tell her, I don't do animals, when all of a sudden Bailey came through loud and clear. I was amazed as he started showing me pictures of his death. I could see that his blood was so very thin and he was bleeding out. I could see him getting weaker and weaker.

My client said that was exactly what had happened. I told her that it felt like some kind of poisoning. My conclusion confirmed what she had already suspected. A neighbor had poisoned her Sweet Bailey.

Bailey taught me some very valuable information as he showed me what happens to animals after they die. I always knew that people go through a life review when they make their transition, but Bailey enlightened me to the fact that animals also go through a form of life review as well. They get to feel the direct results of their interactions with humans. In other words, when animals create pleasure and joy for a human they were connected to, they get to feel that same pleasure and joy as though they were that human. If they caused pain, then they feel that same pain.

It was the most illuminating conversation I have ever had with an animal spirit. Bailey also explained how animals can evolve the same way humans do, and it is possible for them to attain human status. He also assured my client that he would come back to her again. It seems animals reincarnate a bit quicker than humans usually do.

A year or so later, the doctor was going to be in Spokane again. She called to say she had something to show me. There were tears in her eyes when she opened the car door and out jumped this adorable puppy. She said, " I found Bailey. Or should I say he found me." She was so very happy to have her old friend back.

A Fishy Story

Here is an amazing tale told by Laura Lee...you can choose to believe it or not.

In the summer of 2005 one of my best friends passed from this plane to the next. He was a Beta fish I bought as a gift, but he ended up living with me. I named him Drako, and he was one remarkable fish. I would light candles at night and place them by his bowl. Drako would swim around the tiny bowl and then stop to face a candle. He would then stare at it for hours. I called him my "Zen Fishy."

Drako was quite a tough little guy as well as unique, which I would find out later. I didn't really know exactly how to take care of a Beta and was astonished several years later (after he endured temperatures below fifty-five degrees) to find out that Betas were quite temperamental when it came to temperature changes and needed a tropical climate!

Drako stayed in the tiny bowl that he came in for three years because at the time I was too poor to afford anything else for him. My daughter surprised me one summer afternoon when she went to the pet store and bought him a bigger tank from money she had earned working at a car wash. This "new home" was approximately 6 x 5 x 4 inches.

Drako loved his new habitat and enjoyed swimming through the reeds we put in for a symbiotic relationship. Now he was free to roam and would pretend to hide under some of the new plants.

Someone told me if you put a mirror by a Beta, they would flare at it and get ready for a fight. When I tried this on Drako, he just looked at the mirror and then turned away as if to say, "I'm not buying it, and I'm not flaring!" After I had him for a while, I read a Feng Shui book that said you can use a Beta to ward off negative energies. At that point I started to understand what this aquatic friend was **really** doing for me.

This was the same period of time I was trying to help LQ, the young man who was the son of a Cult Lord, get free from his family and the cult. I was bombarded constantly by every kind of dark force, curse, black magick and negative energy you can imagine. I realized that Drako was the "front man" for many psychic assaults meant for me and he was doing an amazing job. I loved that little fish so much, and when I was stressed, it just made me feel better to go to his bowl and watch him swim. He was truly part of the family.

One day I noticed it looked like there was oil at the top of the water in his bowl, so I cleaned it out. The next day I was confused when I noticed the oil was back again. I had a client coming so I thought I would clean it out once more when I was finished.

When the client left, I went to check on Drako and to my dismay, he was floating on his side at the top of the tank. It looked like he might have just crossed over or not quite crossed yet. I ran to the bowl, and cried as I cupped my hand around his little fishy body and started sending him energy. My ex-husband did this once and brought one of our goldfish back to life. I knew if he could do it, for sure I could too!

I started sending Drako life force and electromagnetic energy through my hand when I heard a voice in my head say, "Stop it!" This really startled me, and I looked around thinking I might be doing something wrong. I thought I was just stressed at being in a critical situation, so I took a breath and then proceeded to send more energy. I immediately heard the same voice but this time more powerful, **"Stop it!...Quit doing that! I don't want to be sent back and forced into that sick decrepit body...take your hand away!"**

I slowly removed my hand, wiped the water off, and started to cry. I had been very stressed at the time and this just put me over the edge. I sat on the bed and had a meltdown, staring at the floating fish. All I could do was sob and grieve... one of my best friends and protectors had just crossed over and I felt alone, heartbroken, and guilty for perhaps not taking better care of him.

After ten or fifteen minutes, I starting gaining some composure, and got a tiny zipper baggy to put Drako's body in. I then laid it on my altar, lit a candle on each side and tried to figure out what was going on. It was in this moment of serenity that I heard Drako say to me, "I was your protector for over four years, and now I'm on the other side protecting you from here."

I was overcome with emotion. Turning to look at the little fishy in the baggy on my altar I suddenly heard again, **"Stop looking over there! It's not me. I'm not in that body...**I'm right here next to you!" This kind of disturbed me, but I could see the truth in it. He wasn't there anymore and it was not appropriate to do anything that would project his energy back into that dead body.

Then this amazing fish started to give me a wealth of information about the cosmos and my mission here. I was stunned as I listened to his words of wisdom and council, but every once in a while I would turn and look at the altar in amazement at what was happening.

I would then immediately hear, "Stop looking over there, it's **not** me...I am right here on your left shoulder and that is where I will always be! I am your Dragon guardian, and I have been with you for eons of existence and will be here with you for the remainder of your mission on planet Earth."

When I told my daughter this story, I wasn't sure what she would think, but to my surprise she said, "Duh Mom, his name is **Drako**...of course he's a Dragon!"

It all made perfect sense to me. I have learned a tremendous amount of wisdom from this amazing Dragon spirit who inhabited the little body of a Beta Fish. For over four years he was my guardian in a physical form during some of my darkest hours on this Earth.

You may have heard that Dragons are Wisdom Keepers, and I believe this to be true. Drako has taught me more than words can express, and he continues to be there for me as I do my best to understand and internalize the vastness of Creation.

Got Ghosts???

Got Ghosts???
So What Do You Do Now?

Things That Go Bump in the Night

It is important to remember that not everything that rattles, bumps, creaks, cracks, taps, tones, chimes, sparkles, or shimmers is a ghastly, ghostly night stalker that needs to be evicted. Many, many things can cause *nonsensical noises* and other strange phenomena. Sometimes the visitations are actually Angels, Guardians or Guides watching over you or trying to get your attention. Sometimes electromagnetic fields can cause things to short circuit. Sometimes you may be observing an inter-dimensional shift. And sometimes it could even be your own physical and spiritual vibrations raising to expand into other realms.

We have witnessed a lot of Weird Sh!t, especially if there is an *Indigo Child* or *First Wave Indigo* involved. So, it could possibly be a grand honor for you to be a participant in these strange phenomena.

Ronnie often hears creaking, which sounds exactly like someone is walking in the dining room. It is a much different sound than the other noises she attributes to her new house settling. Just recently she heard a series of tones and when she looked out the window to see if it was the wind chimes, the air was perfectly still. Seeing sparkles of light out of the corner of her eye is a normal occurrence for her.

It is also important to be aware that we are actually sharing this space on Earth with other dimensions and other beings.

It is not illogical to assume that once in a while there is bound to be a "bleed-through." You may be invading their privacy as much as you perceive them to be invading yours.

Just remember, there are many things that can cause bizarre phenomena. If you can stay composed and try to understand that it may not be something out to get you, or a negative situation, you are more likely to find the correct answers and appropriate solutions.

One way to help decide if what you are experiencing is something that needs clearing, is if:

- ~ The hairs on the back of your neck stand up
- ~ There's a puzzling coldness around you or in a specific area
- ~ There are inexplicable obnoxious odors lingering in the air
- ~ Electrical/electronic devices stop working or work intermittently
- ~ Light bulbs frequently need replacing
- ~ Animals are noticeably reacting to something unseen
- ~ Children suddenly become frightened for no apparent reason
- ~ Unusual nightmares are occurring
- ~ You get the **_Hee-Bee-Gee-Bee's_** with a sick feeling in your gut

If it gives you cold pricklies instead of warm fuzzies, it's time to take action!

Rules and Tools for Ghostbusting

Stay Calm

One of the most important things to remember is that *fear* breeds *fear*, so if you can stay calm and go **neutral**, you will be more capable of remedying your predicament... especially when there are children involved. If you do not charge the energy of a haunted place that is already filled with confusion, grief, anger, aggression, anxiety or dread with your own fearful emotions, you will be a lot more in command of the situation. Taking a deep breath, going neutral and using genuine humor and laughter when you are confronted with a phenomenon that gives you *"the creeps"* will be your best tool for keeping your wits about you.

Staying calm is like putting on a "Teflon coating" so this W.S. won't stick to you and make *you* a part of *it*. Many negative energies and entities feed on fear and will do their best to exacerbate the situation. Hang a sign in your mind that says, *"Don't Feed the Animals!"* It will remind you that *you* are in control.

Remember the Acronym:
False Evidence Appearing Real = FEAR

On most occasions when we are called to do a clearing, our clients are terrified because they feel that the ghosts or entities causing all the problems are **EVIL**. Many times their own fears and misperceptions magnify the energy so that it appears to be even more hostile, aggressive, and downright horrifying. However, these lost and trapped souls are actually quite confused themselves, and are almost always suffering from terrible guilt, anger or inferiority complexes that are ego-based, causing them to lash out. This may sound funny, but it is true!

Ronnie always makes it a point to share her belief with our clients. Her Angels call it the **Godness of Being**. "Everyone and everything is a part of God, and when you truly know this, there is no reason to be afraid of anything."

In fact, physics is now catching up with metaphysics. Since the invention of the electron microscope, some amazing truths have been discovered:

1. Nothing is solid. In others words, there are spaces between the atoms of everything in existence. About 95% of physical matter is space.

2. Everything in our Universe vibrates.

On a local TV show, Ronnie heard Dannion Brinkley explain that quantum physicists have discovered a base component of the Universe. It is literally the fabric that holds everything together, the space between the atoms. They call it, "the exotic-exo-nano-sphere." The most astounding thing about this base component is that it vibrates to the exact same frequency as **LOVE**. So, Love is actually the glue or fabric that binds us all together along with everything else in existence. (We hippies had it right all along!) Now, in Ronnie's mind, another word for Love is **GOD**. Thus, God is within ***everything***, literally. Her favorite Ghostbuster Gal quote is, ***"There is NO thing that is NOT God."*** When you totally embrace this reality of Oneness, there is no fear. That is why Ronnie can do her work with Love, compassion and humor.

Laura Lee has a different perspective on how this Universe works, and tries to redefine all the mis-perceptions and propaganda regarding the concept and the word "God." She uses love and compassion intertwined with a no-nonsense approach in handling the scoundrels of the Universe. She believes there are entities and energies inside this Universe that have been corrupted and do not respond to love. Therefore, they need to be handled from a different angle. With both approaches, Laura Lee and Ronnie truly have all the bases covered!

Raising Vibration

One of the easiest ways to raise your own vibration is through breathing. We are not talking about the shallow chest breathing that most people are used to, but the deep belly breathing that an infant does. It certainly helps to breathe with intention as well. Imagine that you are breathing in the Loving Light of the Universe and releasing any stress, tension or fear. The higher your vibration, the less likely a negative being would want to hang around you. Fear, hate, anger, jealousy, revenge, guilt, low self-esteem all create a propensity to lower vibration. Thoughts of love, compassion, peace, laughter and deep breathing serve to raise it.

Now that you understand how to raise your own vibration, it is important that you pay attention to your environment. When you raise the vibration of your space to a high enough level, and sustain that level for a long enough time, an entity will either conform to this new level and then be able to "see the Light" when you ask your guides or Angels to assist you...or, they will maintain their lower vibration and be so uncomfortable with the surroundings that they will have to leave. Maintaining this level of high vibration may be difficult if you have an "anger management problem" or a problem with substance addiction.

Here are a few things that might be of assistance in your quest to raise your vibration as well as the vibration of the place that is being haunted. When we do ghostbustings, we take some of these items with us, and fondly refer to them as our **"Ghostbusting Paraphernalia."**

It is imperative when you use these methods, your intent be sincere and focused. We always ask the Angels and our Guardians to be present to assist in removing any trapped souls or negative energies that do not belong, affirming that the **highest good** be served. These are the prerequisites before attempting any ghostbusting. You will see these concepts repeated again and again throughout the various techniques we have presented.

Ghostbusting Paraphernalia

Many different methods and tools are available to help clear your space. Here are just a few that we use, along with some suggestions on how to apply them. *The most important thing to keep in mind when performing a clearing ceremony is to have an unwavering, positive intent, with love and respect for all life forms involved.* When you have this attitude of compassionate power, you have already taken a big chunk out of your task.

Prayers of Protection

Before you commence working with the paranormal, it is important to remember to protect yourself from the influence and presence of **uninvited guests**.

Here are some prayers that Ronnie has been using for years that work well for her. If you don't have one of your own that you are confident about, you can try these. As we have said before, it is the intent and the emotions behind the words that are important. We also believe that God-Creator, is not judgmental as to what name you use when addressing the Supreme Being, only that you use respect and pure intent. These prayers can be of great value in creating a feeling of calmness and focus as you prepare to cleanse your environment and make it a safe place to dwell. These prayers are just a model, so fill in the blank with whatever spiritual power resonates with you. (*God/Goddess, Lord/Lady, Jesus, Buddha, Krishna, Father/Mother, Creator, Great Spirit, Allah, Source, Universe, etc.*) The words in parentheses are what Ronnie uses.

PRAYERS OF PROTECTION

I AM THE LOVING LIGHT OF (GOD) _____
(CREATOR) _____ PLEASE PLACE YOUR
PROTECTIVE GOLDEN LIGHT
AROUND ME THIS DAY AND NIGHT

AND A PROTECTIVE (CROSS OF JESUS CHRIST & STAR
OF DAVID) _____
(*Name the symbol you deem to be the
greatest protection and power, i.e.;
Five Pointed Star, Merkaba, Kryahgenetics Egg, Ankh*)
ACROSS MY SOLAR PLEXUS.

IN THE NAME OF (**GOD**) _____
IF YOU ARE NOT OF PURE LOVE
AND PURE LIGHT
YOU MUST LEAVE **NOW**
SEEK YOUR OWN LEVEL
NEVER TO RETURN
IN THE NAME OF (*THE FATHER, THE SON,
AND THE HOLY SPIRIT*) _____

SO BE IT!

THE LIGHT OF GOD IS WITHIN ME
THE LOVE OF GOD ENFOLDS ME
THE PRESENCE OF GOD WATCHES OVER ME
AND THE POWER OF GOD PROTECTS ME
WHEREVER I AM, GOD IS
I AM THE LOVING LIGHT OF GOD

SO BE IT!

CLEANSING PRAYER

To be used with purification substances such as: sage, water, salt, incense, frankincense, myrrh, rose oil spray, a flame, etc.

(CREATOR)_____

PLEASE CLEANSE AND CLEAR THIS
(*property, room, crystal, jewelry, divination tool, etc.*)

OF ANY AND ALL DARKNESS AND NEGATIVITY.

ALLOW ONLY THE HIGHEST
VIBRATIONS OF LOVE

(LIGHT, LAUGHTER, CLARITY, PROTECTION)

TO BE PRESENT

THANK YOU

SO BE IT!

~ ~ ~ ~ ~

Laura Lee uses other protective protocols such as: The Kryahgenetics Egg and the Aulmauracite stone of truth to establish a stronger link to her Higher Self. (Continue reading this chapter for further explanation.) She also uses a specific meditation to amp up her Core Star. (See FirstWaveIndigo.com for instructions.)

Laura Lee calls on her Spirit Guides and Guardians (including her Dragons and Gargoyles) to protect her.

Kryahgenetics Egg

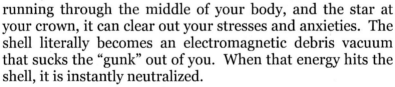

This is a picture of the Kryahgenetics Egg that is on the cover of Laura Lee's book, *Kryahgenetics, The Simple Secrets of Human Alchemy*. Some very complex and powerful, ancient encoded healing symbols are implanted in this Egg.

We have found that if you meditate using this egg, by imagining yourself inside, with the center D.N.A. helix running through the middle of your body, and the star at your crown, it can clear out your stresses and anxieties. The shell literally becomes an electromagnetic debris vacuum that sucks the "gunk" out of you. When that energy hits the shell, it is instantly neutralized.

We also use the Egg as a protection tool in our ghostbustings. We have discovered that negative and hostile energies/entities find it very difficult to penetrate the shell because it neutralizes them too, and they will eventually give up. The protective qualities of this Egg seem to last about twelve hours, so if you set one up before you go to sleep, it will last through the night. Whenever we have used these Eggs, we feel warm and fuzzy inside. Perhaps it's reminiscent of the feeling we had being in a safe warm womb. The sacred geometry infused throughout this symbol seems to have technology that is very advanced. The Egg has been a very powerful mechanism for us, and there are still many things we are learning about this marvelous device.

Music

Music and tones can do some amazing things to shift the energy in any environment.

Here is a partial list of music we use to raise vibration:

> ***The Lost Chord*** by Jonathon Goldman
> ***Millennium*** by Crosswynd
> ***Light Reiki Touch*** by Merlin's Magic
> ***Company of Angels*** by Robin Miller
> ***Transcendence*** by Robin Miller
> ***Gifts of Angels*** by Stephen Halpern
> ***Angels of the Deep*** by Raphael
> ***Light of Midnight*** by Ed Van Fleet
> ***Healing*** by Anugama
> ***Troika Series*** by David Arkenstone
> ***Heart & Genesis*** by Barry Goldstein
> ***Magic Carpet*** by David Michael & Randy Mead
> ***Surrender*** by Stephen Pike
> ***Through the Stargate*** by Constance Demby

Salt

Because of the electrolytic effects of salt, this mineral provides a great tool to pull/draw negative energy to it. You can put it in little dishes in all four corners of a room or a house and replace it after twenty-four hours for at least three days. Some people will put a line of salt around the outside of their homes. State your intent as you place the salt. When employing this tool, you must be cautious to make sure you use it with pure intent. When disposing of it, do so with the intent to neutralize it before you bury it in the Earth or wrap it up in plastic or saran wrap and send it to the city dump.

Salt can be used in a shower by rubbing it all over to get psychic debris off your body and out of your auric field. In clearing crystals, set your intention as you put them in a small bowl filled with salt. Let them sit overnight.

Bells, Bowls, Tuning Forks & Drums

The pitch, tone, vibration, and clarity of certain bells, crystal bowls, tuning forks and drums will help change the energetics of a room or space, and bring the vibration to a higher octave. This by itself with pure intent may be enough to clear your affected area of negative energy, but it will not be effective for actual ghosts.

Crystals

Ronnie is a quartz crystal fanatic. She has more than a thousand of them all over her house and property, of various shapes and sizes. When using crystals in ghostbusting or any other spiritual endeavor, it is important that they be cleansed before and after each use. Crystals can be placed in sunlight or moonlight to intensify their strength.

Strictly speaking, crystals, on their own, do not contain any "magical powers." They do, however, amplify energy and can be programmed for specific applications. Once you know the proper method you can infuse them with the power of: protection, clarity, healing, angelic connection, Loving Light radiance, etc.

All crystals are not created equal. They each have their own forte. Some crystals are cut in sacred geometric patterns to further amplify the energy. Ronnie uses one in the shape of a Star of David for all her readings and ghostbustings, along with a piece of Aulmauracite rock.

Holy Water

There are two types of Holy Water. The traditional water can be obtained at a Catholic church. It is water that has been specifically blessed by a priest, and can be most effective in chasing away dark spirits. The other type of water can be made by you, or someone else. There are books with recipes for Holy Water that are very efficient for eliminating unwanted disincarnated guests. We have an intense full moon ceremony that will create very powerful Holy Water imbued with sacred energies from Earth, Angelic and Cosmic Realms. It is very important to remember as in all your ghostbusting attempts that intention and prayer are your main ingredients. Unfortunately we have found that Holy Water is a temporary fix and ghosts only leave for a short period of time before they are back again, raising unholy Hell.

Rose Water

Rose oil mixed with purified water and put in a spray bottle can do wonders to raise the vibration of a room. Just spray the "affected area" and set your intent in a similar manner as smudging. Rose oil has one of the highest vibrations of any oil. Ronnie brings an atomizer of rose oil to all our ghostbustings.

Smudging

Smudging is the act of using the smoke of sacred plants such as; dried Sage, Sweet Grass, Lavender, Pine Resin, Copal, Temple Incense such as Nag Champa, or any other purification substance. The smoke has properties of removing heavy, negative, hostile energy and raising the vibration to a higher octave. In some cases, if your intent is pure, this can clear many types of negative energies from your environment and your own auric field.

1. To begin, take some deep breaths and calm yourself. (This would be a good time to use the Kryahgenetics Egg.)

2. Call in your unseen helpers. Then hold the intent that the highest good be served.

3. As you light the smudging substance, you might want to start by acknowledging the plant you are using for its assistance, and offer your feelings of gratitude. The plant kingdom is very powerful, and if you align yourself with that energy, it will help you get in touch with the wonders of creation. This alone will change the energy in the room. If you have a feather fan, that will help you direct the smoke. If not, you can make one out of paper or even use your hand. As you direct the smoke, recite the cleansing prayer or make up one of your own.

Many traditions begin by directing smoke to the four directions: North, South, East and West. This gives them homage and honor.

As you cleanse the area, work methodically from one end to the other. Ronnie was taught to smudge in a clockwise direction, while other traditions may smudge counter clockwise. Do whatever feels right for your situation. **Remember**, *you can't go wrong if your intent is right*.

Be sure to get all the dark places, i.e.; under the beds, in the closets, behind furniture, in back of the furnace and water heater, etc. Make sure that all corners are smudged top to bottom. When you are finished, put out the smudge (some indigenous people bury the residue in the Earth), again thank the plants you've used, and give gratitude to the Creator and Angelic helpers for assisting in purifying your space.

Aulmauracite: The Magical Mystical Stone of Truth & Justice

We use this rock in **every** one of our ghostbustings. (Laura Lee also uses it with Kryahgenetics, her custom designed healing techniques.) In fact, it is now **mandatory** for clients to have a small grid of these rocks around their house before we will do a ghostbusting. It makes our job so much easier! Without the grid, it's like walking through Jell-O. We have to expend five times the energy to extract the information from the unseen world, leaving us exhausted.

This power rock is one of Laura Lee's best friends, and helps her find the truth in the mysteries that lay in her path. One of the things that makes this rock so nice to work with is that unlike crystals, it does not need to be cleansed, (it is self-cleaning!) Laura Lee has used it in dealing with some pretty nasty dark forces and curses, and feels that it has literally saved her life on several occasions. One such life-saving incident happened in July of 1996. Here is Laura Lee's rendition of that story.

It was about ten days before Lee Carol and Jan Tobar came to Spokane to do a Kryon Channeling. (Kryon is the non-physical Magnetic Master who speaks through Lee Carol.) I was hosting and producing that event and had a million things to get accomplished in a short amount of time. The phone rang about 7:00 a.m. awakening me from a sound sleep. Turning over in bed, I reached out to put an end to the annoying ringing. Instantly, I got this horrendous rush of dizziness like I have never felt in my entire life. This was not some wimpy little dizzy, spacey feeling, but more like an inner and outer force that felt as if something was throwing me across the bed!

I struggled to talk coherently, but had to hang up quickly. I knew something was terribly wrong. Lying there, I tried to gain some composure and examine the situation, but it was really difficult. If I moved my head, my arms, legs, or even my eyes in anything other than super slow motion, I felt as though I was not only being flung across the room, but spinning as I flew! The slightest motion would start this reaction, and it was all I could do to keep my wits about me. It was terrifying! I was completely immobilized. I had so much that needed to be done, and most of the things could not be delegated. I just could **not** be put out of commission now! All I could do was lay there, breathe slowly, and try to keep myself from going insane, literally.

Thank goodness I had enough sense to grab my power rock. As I clutched it to my chest, I cried for help. Immediately, I did a scan on my body to see what the cause of this bizarre and senseless condition was. I scanned over and over to see if it was some sort of nutritional deficiency. I found a slight potassium deficit, but nothing that would cause this!

I managed to call my husband and told him I needed help. Realizing I was in serious trouble, he brought me every herbal remedy he could think of. He smudged the room, and did repeated reflexology treatments on my feet, but nothing would touch this horrifying condition. It felt like I was going to die! I could actually feel my life force getting pulled out of me and it was more frightening than anything I had ever experienced.

The only thing that could possibly cause such a condition was some sort of black magic, dark sorcery, curse...or possibly hostile radionics. I knew I was being dealt a deathblow, and I knew I had to do something or it would take me out. I had a pretty good idea who and what was behind it, and part of the reason was to put a damper on the seminar I was arranging...but it went far beyond that...it was a personal assault, and I knew it! That, in and of itself, made me want to cry. I couldn't believe anyone would purposefully do something like this to me.

My heroes at that time were the Care Bears. I bought the kids all their movies, their books, their stuffed animals, and I was trying my hardest to make my home a "care-a-lot" on Earth. It absolutely short-circuited my brain to think that someone or something out there would be so hostile and vindictive. I had never done any dark sorcery or dark magic in my life, and it boggled my mind to think that someone else would consciously do this hideous thing to another person.

The only thing I could do to maintain any kind of inner and outer balance was to lie perfectly still, and breathe very slowly. I held the large power rock to my chest and solicited its help, and the help of every benevolent power I could manifest. After several hours of this, my vertigo had let up only slightly, and then returned.

I was a little concerned that these bizarre symptoms were not being overthrown by my heartfelt pleas to the Universal Powers. *How could this be happening to me?* After many hours of this nightmare, I decided I'd better go visit the bathroom before my bladder burst. I crawled into the bathroom and, being the independent gal that I was, didn't ask for any help. **Big** mistake. It felt like some force was throwing me into the side of the bathtub and **wham**, I conked my head a good one, and thought I'd lose consciousness in this most vulnerable position. So, now I'm not only dizzy, but I have a splitting headache! Somehow I got back to my bed and started to sob...but that wasn't good either because even that movement made me dizzy!

I managed through the next seventy-two hours and the vertigo finally started easing up enough so that I could go places. However, if I moved my head back even slightly, I would go into a spin. I remember being in a ceramics shop and tilting my head back to look at one of the upper shelves. Instantly, I got a dizzy flash that nearly threw me against a shelf filled with delicate items. I knew I was in a very precarious position and decided I'd better just sit down right where I was, in the middle of the aisle, to prevent any costly accidents. When I regained my equilibrium, I sheepishly made a quick exit to save myself from further embarrassment.

I continued to do everything I could think of, smudging, putting salt in the corners, lighting candles, and on and on. Now, here is the strange thing. I took the opportunity to leave town for a few days on four separate occasions. A pattern started taking shape. My symptoms took about forty-eight hours before they started to subside, and after seventy-two hours, the symptoms were gone. When I returned home, however, within twelve hours the symptoms would return. This happened until I moved from that house six months later...and since then those dizzy spells have ceased.

On reflection of this entire episode in my life, I went into meditation and asked my Aulmauracite rock why it didn't help me. Why did it allow this magnetic glitch in my brain to take place? I had asked with all my heart for it to bring me back to balance and eliminate this curse, this hex, this hideous encounter with some unseen force or whatever the heck it was.

Then with absolute calmness, serenity and love, I received my answer. The Aulmauracite **was** helping me, **and it was doing an impeccable job, as were my spiritual helpers.** I was informed that the intense, focused energies that targeted and descended upon me were designed not only to temporarily immobilize me, but to do a permanent job as well. One that would in a short time put me six feet under and out of the game of Earth life permanently, leaving my four children without a mother. I know now, without a doubt, that this is true, and the intelligence and light within the Aulmauracite Rock had protected me and helped me stabilize when I was supposed to be engulfed in terror and overpowering despair.

This is just one of the numerous times when my beloved rock friend, *Aulmauracite* has been there for me. There are many other instances this rock came to my rescue when dark forces were at work trying to make my life a living hell. Now, I don't leave home without it.

You can find more information about this power rock on Laura Lee's website: www.mistychouse.com/Aurauralite/Aurauralite-toc.htm

Here are excerpts from Laura Lee's books about Aulmauracite:

Scientific Qualities
Some of the scientific qualities we have discovered about this rock have been absolutely astounding. It has properties that are literally, **"Out Of This World."**

- ~ Assay testing revealed that Aulmauracite is 58% iron (in a form that *does not* oxidize/rust.) The remaining 42% consists of seventy-two other elements, including all the noble metals (plus some that are foreign to this planet!) It appears that the ratio of these elements in relationship to each other gives this power rock its unusual properties.

- ~ It has its own power source and its own ground. There is nothing in our world like this.

~ It is a high-powered broadcaster that beefs up the volume of whatever you're trying to broadcast, whether a desire or intention, or whether it's being used to amplify Tesla technology.

~ It custom-designs itself to the user to assist them with their benevolent intentions.

~ When someone tries to use it for unethical or **un-loving** purposes...it has its own internal ethical code and will shut off its power and go *temporarily dormant.* **It won't get involved!**

~ It puts its owner or user on their *best destiny path,* which almost always alters their lives, and brings about some very dramatic changes when they get their rock!

~ When you pass it around a room full of people, the power rock won't pick up and hold psychic debris like crystals do. Instead it neutralizes the negativity and grounds it out, therefore it doesn't need cleansing. It's extremely "user friendly."

~ Aulmauracite is a very intelligent rock, but *You* and *Your Higher Self* are the power source that activates its energies...it simply will wait for you to give it a job, and the more you use it, the happier it is, and the better it works.

~ Sometimes you may not know when you give it a job...some of its commands may come directly from your Higher Self and you may not be aware of it immediately. For instance, when most people pick it up, it usually goes to work balancing their energy and holographic fields, opening up their psychic centers, and when they begin to work with it, they automatically lock on to their best destiny paths!

- It doesn't like to be encased in plastic or synthetic material because that smothers it and therefore, deadens its signal.

- When you acquire one of these rocks or the dust (Aurauralite), truth automatically begins to surface and manifest in your life.

The following information was taken from Laura Lee's web site.

Having worked with this cosmic rock for several years, I have some astounding tales to tell. About a year ago I took the rock to a friend of mine who is a Tesla scientist. I told him about some of the experiences I had with the rock, its broadcasting capabilities, and how it has its own grounding system.

He responded the way a lot of men do the first time I present them with this amazing rock and try to explain its vastness in two or three minutes (while they are only half listening and the other half patronizing me). I knew he was very skeptical about what he called the "New Age Rock" I was showing him, but he did give me the courtesy of saying he would like to conduct some experiments on it with some of his equipment. Of course, I had no problem with this, as I was also curious as to how the rock would stand up to some additional hard core 3-D testing.

To begin with, he wanted to find out what would happen when he ran electrical current through it to see what its conduction capabilities were. He first ran A.C. current into the rock and nothing happened...no reading on the meter. So, next he ran D.C. current through it...and zip, zero, nothing was reading. At this point he kept testing other materials to make sure there wasn't anything wrong with his meter. With this rock's high iron content it didn't make much sense that he couldn't pick up a reading! Next he tried running different sound frequencies through it, but again... no meter reading! Still wondering if there was something wrong with his equipment he kept checking and rechecking it with other materials to make sure his equipment wasn't malfunctioning.

After this, he decided to run light pulses through the rock and once again...no reading! At this point I suggested that he take the grounding wire off and see what happens. He looked at me like, *this is an absolutely unfounded, asinine request, and you really don't have a clue about what you're asking, but I'll patronize you and do it anyway...***but not before I check my equipment again for a short or some other defect.**

After checking his light pulse machine thoroughly, he ran the pulses through the rock again ...no meter reading. Then he took the grounding wire off as I had suggested and his eyes got so big they darn near bugged out of their sockets! He said, "Well I'll be darned (only he didn't say *darned*), this thing has its own ground! How can that be? I've never seen anything like it...It has its own ground!" I said, "I know, that's what I've been trying to tell you!" Then he looked me square in the eye and said, "Where did this rock come from? Where the heck is this thing getting its ground? What's going on here?" I replied, "I told you it wasn't from around here. Now do you believe me?"

With that, he went to work rechecking to see if the sound and electrical current would show up on the meter without the ground...but again, no readings. The only reading he was able to get was with light pulses and the grounding wire disconnected. According to the science of our Universe this was virtually impossible!

Draw your own conclusions as to what the implications are here, and what it means. I know for me it was extremely validating, but to my scientist friend it was very unsettling to have a substance that defied some of the laws of physics that had heretofore been so cut and dried. And I have to admit, it was amusing to me to see his left brain try to rationalize and figure out **what in the world** was going on with this "New

Age Rock." Ironically, you would have to go **out of this world,** to get your answers!

Aulmauracite Grid

Small Aulmauracite grid rocks can be placed in rooms, houses, yards, towns, cities etc., to stabilize the area and create a new matrix. To set up a five stone Power Grid, place a rock in each corner and one in the center, or as close to the center as possible. Once the four corners of the power grid have been put in place, hold the fifth or center rock and give the grid whatever commands you feel appropriate: bring truth, justice, peace, prosperity, protection, clearing, healing, etc.

Then tell the grid to "turn on" as you place the center stone. You can instantly feel it charging up and creating an energy of stability and clarity. These little stones come in colorful tissue paper so you won't accidentally vacuum them up if you place them on the floor. Many people thumbtack them to the wall or ceiling.

These grid stones are small but powerful, and remember size does not matter. Just ask Ronnie.

New Technology

One of the tools that Ronnie has found helpful in exercising her psychic muscle and in communicating with non-physical spirits is a program called PATHS: **P**rograms **A**uthoring **T**he **H**uman **S**ubconscious. It is a revolutionary new technology that helps to rewire the sub-conscious mind for whatever is desired. There are programs for increasing intuition, unconditional Love, growing closer to God, as well as other

Spiritual enhancements. They also include a free sleep booster to help recharge after doing Spirit work. www.paths2connectedness.com

When in Rome...

It is important to remember that in many cases, if trapped souls do not recognize the entity that comes to their rescue, they may not leave. So, it is critical to be able to relate to ghosts on their own level, or as they say, "When in Rome do as the Romans do."

Ronnie has a fascinating story that illustrates this principle when she was asked to clear the outside of the Glover Mansion to facilitate a quick sale. It had been on the market for a *very* long time.

I was getting ready to embark on my first solo ghostbusting, when I was prompted by my Angels to bring a sacred Native American medicine necklace made specifically for me by a Cheyenne man, along with a bowl of sage. Thinking this was a rather odd request, I began to argue with them (as I sometimes do). I did not want to look like a fool wearing this big showy necklace out in public. After much debate with my very gracious and patient allies, I finally surrendered (as I always do), and brought the prescribed tools with me. It was a good thing too!

Arriving at the mansion, I was a little apprehensive. This was all so new to me and I had no idea what I was getting myself into. However, since my Angels had chimed in so insistently before I even got there, I figured I could count on their guidance. I was right.

As I began my preparation, I started receiving step-by-step instructions from my Heavenly Helpers. The first thing I was told to do was mix some of the earth I was standing on, in my sage bowl. This was a totally new concept for me.

Then came the directive I was absolutely dreading. I was told to **put on the sacred medicine necklace**. Feeling very self-conscious with Neila, the owner staring at me, I took a deep breath and complied. The smudge bowl was then lit, prayers were said and after cleansing myself, I slowly began to walk around the mansion.

Neila pointed out an area below the home where she had sensed something strange. As I walked down the narrow path I started to "see" pictures in my mind's eye of an Indian village. It was a happy time, children were playing in the stream and the hustle and bustle of women going about their daily activities permeated the scene. All of a sudden, it was gone. No movement, nothing. I wasn't sure what had happened, but as I continued my investigation it didn't take long to find out.

Walking back up the hill, I came to a place where I perceived a powerful energy vortex. Neila felt it too. I centered myself, took some deep breaths and smudged the area with sage. There before me appeared the Chief of this tribe. It was quite incredible. As his awareness of me intensified, he was awestruck. I began communicating with him telepathically, and he was humbled by my presence. He actually thought I was some kind of God.

The Chief then proceeded to go down on one knee, with his head bent, and would not even look at me. I was quite perplexed and a little embarrassed. This certainly was a first. I couldn't figure out what would cause such a reaction. Asking him to get up, I told him that I wasn't a God, but someone who was sent by Great Spirit to help him. He replied, "Only a God would have such powerful medicine." It was then I realized why I was told to wear the sacred necklace. If I did not have it on, I truly believe this Chief would not have given me the time of day. It was the energy of the necklace that was recognized by this soul.

I began to receive the pictures of the Chief's story and why he was still here. Many, many years ago, he was the leader of the village I had seen below the home. One terrible day, this village was attacked by a very large group of white men on horseback. Most of the fighting took place behind what is now the mansion. Great numbers of men, women and children were massacred because the white men wanted the land. The braves fought valiantly, but the village was outnumbered. The Chief felt so helpless and guilty as he watched his people die brutally.

Believing that his medicine was weak, when the Chief finally succumbed, he chose not to join with Great Spirit because he was unworthy. He was unable to protect his people and save them from the slaughter. And so, there he stayed in his anguish and shame. That is until I came along. I found out his name was Walking Two Sticks. Apparently, he used to use two large sticks as he walked up and down the hills of his village.

Gently, I informed the Chief that it was time for him to move on and Great Spirit and the Grandfathers were awaiting him. I assured him that it was not because his medicine was weak, but because the other's medicine was too strong. That's why the massacre occurred. There was nothing more he could have done. A beautiful tunnel of energy formed and the Chief was finally ready to let go of his guilt and unworthiness. He headed into the tunnel with tears of relief in his eyes and was embraced by the welcoming Love of the Creator. Guiding the Chief back "home" was a very powerful experience, but there was much more work ahead.

Expecting to see more Native Americans, I was quite surprised when the next trapped soul I came across was a little boy. Wearing a white shirt and black knickers, he looked to be about four years old. He was amazed that I could communicate with him. We were standing near the front of the mansion and I saw the boy look up.

As I connected with him on a deeper level, he began to show me his story. Numerous times he had been told by his parents not to play near the bedroom windows on the top floor. They were rather large, opened outward, and had no screens. One day, out of curiosity, coupled with thinking he was grown up enough, this precious little boy, dared to go where no child should have gone. Consequently, as he was looking down, he lost his balance and fell to his death. His last thoughts were, "Mummy and Daddy won't love me anymore. I'm bad." The overwhelming guilt and heavy negative emotions kept him trapped, right where he died.

My Angels guided me to bring his mother and father back through the tunnel to arrange a reunion, so they could welcome their son "home." And what a glorious homecoming it was! As the child saw his parents, he gleefully ran to meet them.

The most extraordinary thing about this ghostbusting experience was that after the boy joined his parents, he turned around to wave goodbye and said, "Thank you." Believe it or not, he was one of the few ghosts to actually take the time to offer a word of gratitude. It brought tears to my eyes and a wonderfully warm feeling to my heart.

Moving on, I approached the back of the mansion. As I went up behind the house, smudging all the way, I could see the trapped souls of Chief Walking Two Sticks' braves. They were scattered over the hillside. None of them had felt worthy enough to join the Grandfathers. I saw how courageously they fought but were annihilated by the men on horseback. I felt their shock and sheer terror as they heard the earsplitting blasts of the "thundersticks" the men carried. Confusion was a huge part of their turmoil as they fell down dead without ever being touched by a human hand.

Surveying the area, I noticed that all the souls were men, except one. Curled up in a ball next to one of the braves, was a young woman. She had not been murdered by the marauding invaders. Surviving the attack, she had wandered through the bloody carnage in a state of shock and utter disbelief. Upon finding her dead husband's body, she was so grief-stricken that she simply positioned herself next to him and willed her spirit to leave.

Feeling a bit overwhelmed myself from this emotional onslaught, with the help of my Angels, I opened a tunnel of Light, and invited the group of bewildered souls to go "home." There was a great deal of hesitation at first. They, like the Chief, felt they needed to stay and protect the land because their medicine was not strong enough for them to join the Great Spirit. Unruffled, I let them know that it was time to go. Again the energy of the necklace came through for me. I explained that their Chief felt it was okay to leave and was waiting for them. That's all it took, and the procession through the tunnel began.

The area felt so much lighter after my work was completed. With this incredible experience behind me, I went home to ponder just what had taken place. I seemed to have a knack for this sort of thing, and my awareness and understanding had expanded greatly. I also knew I could trust and count on my Angelic helpers to support me in this calling. I realized how important it was to relate to ghosts on their own level, speaking their own language. All in all, it had been a very successful day.

As a side note, Neila received a contract on the mansion one week after this clearing. As fate would have it, a few months later the deal fell through, and that allowed The Ghostbuster Gals to finish the ghastly ghost deportation ***inside*** the infested walls. (See Chapter 11 *The Torture Room* for the rest of the story.)

Do-it-Yourself Ghostbusting Guide

Now that you have read about the rules and tools that can be used to eliminate unsolicited "guests," and know how to protect yourself while doing it, we can give you a step-by-step protocol of how to execute your very own ghostbusting. It is imperative to remember that intention is everything. The stronger and more positive your intent, the better the results.

To prepare, set a sacred space for yourself, open your heart and ask for guidance with sincerity and reverence. Call upon your Creator and your unseen partners for their assistance. Then trust that you will be successful.

1. Put on some vibration raising music.

2. Light a candle while setting your intention.

3. Take some deep calming, cleansing breaths to raise your own vibration.

4. Place yourself and your environment in a Kryahgenetics egg.

5. Do your prayers of protection.

6. Smudge yourself and the area in which you are working (Sage, Holy Water, Rose Oil, etc.)

7. Take some deep breaths and ask for Angelic assistance to create a portal, or tunnel of light nearby. Visualize it.

8. Ask the proper spiritual authority to assist these "*lost souls*" back to the Light. If you have certain guides or

Angels that you trust, invite them in to assist you. Two of the many beings we usually call upon from the Spiritual Hierarchy are, Jeshua Ben Joseph (Jesus/Sananda) and Archangel Michael. They seem to be a main component in our clearings. We have also invoked: Raphael, Gabriel, Metatron, Kryon, Buddha, St. Germain, White Buffalo Calf Woman, Quan Yin, as well as others spiritual authority figures to support us. On some occasions Laura Lee has even requested the Benevolent Dragon and Gargoyle Realms to assist.

9. Imagine any energy/entity that is foreign to your environment being escorted into the portal.

10. See the portal closing behind itself and feel the energy being whisked away.

11. Thank the Angels, etc. for their help.

12. Blow out the candle and congratulate yourself on a job well done.

13. Keep yourself and your environment in a protective Egg for three days because there may be some residual energy.

Know that if you feel this is too difficult to handle, or you did not remove all of ghastly ghosts and negative W.S., you can call us for help.

* Remember, it is not good to have any ghosts around for any reason.

Suggested Reading List

These are some of the books that have been extremely influential in our lives as well as our work.

Living in an Indigo House	Laura Lee Mistycah
Conversations with God-Books 1 & 3	Neale Donald Walsch
Saved by the Light	Dannion Brinkley
At Peace in the Light	Dannion Brinkley
Secrets of the Light	Dannion & Kathryn Brinkley
Jewels for the Soul	Kathryn Brinkley
Emissary of Light	James Twyman
Emissary of Love	James Twyman
The Moses Code	James Twyman
Celestine Prophecy	James Redfield
Talking to Heaven	James Van Praagh
Healing Grief	James Van Praagh
Ghosts Among Us	James Van Praagh
Return of Merlin	Deepak Chopra
Walking Between the Worlds	Gregg Braden
Awakening to Zero Point	Gregg Braden
The Isaiah Effect	Gregg Braden
Animal Speak	Ted Andrews
The Lost Chord	Jonathan Goldman
Seth Speaks	Jane Roberts
The Oversoul Seven Trilogy	Jane Roberts
On the Wings of Heaven	G.W. Hardin
Hear All Creatures	Karen Anderson
The Quantum Key	Aaron Murakami
The Secret	Rhonda Byrne
The New Earth	Eckhart Tolle
Zero Degrees of Separation	Sandra Hatfield
Conspiracies and Secret Societies (plus any books by)	Brad & Sherry Steiger

Successful Adventures in Ghost Deportation

Glover Mansion...
The Continuing Saga of Ronnie's First Official Ghostbusting

Who's Afraid of the Big Bad Basement?

Everyone was afraid to go into the basement at Glover Mansion. If one of the staff had to go down there, they **never** went alone.

When Neila, the owner, had my friend Anya come to clear the mansion (and I tagged along), she made sure that after we had worked on the upstairs, we went into the dreaded basement.

As we walked down the stairs, the atmosphere became heavier and heavier. It was so creepy, it made the hairs stand up on the back of our necks, and we got goose bumps.

There was something "rotten" in that basement and we could feel it. The sense of anxiety was almost overwhelming. It crystallized in my mind what the word haunted really meant. The energy was so disquieting and full of apprehension it completely unnerved us. No wonder people got out of there as quickly as they could.

Taking some deep breaths, Anya and I, with the help of the Angels, went about opening a tunnel of Light. Suddenly, I perceived movement...lots of movement! The lost and trapped souls were coming out of their hiding places and gathering in front of the energy field before them.

What shocked me the most was that these ghosts were actually very timid. In fact, they were more afraid of us than we were of them! Leading the group of souls was a man in his twenties wearing a white shirt with rolled up sleeves. He had thick green suspenders holding up dark green woolen trousers. A large beige padded cap topped his head. He held his young daughter in his arms as his wife stood by his side. I could see the trepidation in his eyes, as he looked around hesitantly. Telepathically, I reached out to him letting him know it was okay to go into the Light, and he and his family would be safe and protected. With that, he took the first step in, and the others followed. It was quite a procession. Ghosts were coming out from every nook and cranny, excited for the opportunity to finally go "home."

Anya and I discovered that there was a negative energy vortex in the basement. The mansion was located in close proximity to a hospital. Because of all the violence and tyranny that had taken place in the house, it held a very low vibration. When people in the hospital died in extreme shock, fear, anger, etc., they found themselves drawn to the mansion to settle with the rest of the trapped spirits. The Universal Law of **like attracts like** certainly did apply here.

Once all the souls went through the tunnel and were where they belonged, Anya and I said a prayer for them and sealed up the portal. We were all astounded at how much lighter and brighter it now felt in the basement.

I am happy to report that after this major ghost deportation, the staff no longer has a problem with the basement. The energy feels fine, and the fear was completely eradicated.

The Torture Room

Years later, there were more disturbances at the mansion. By that time, the ghostbusting business was up and running so The Ghostbuster Gals took on the rest of the ghastly, ghoulish garbage. This was stuff that was buried many layers deep in the mansion's foundation. It took numerous hours of clambering around in the huge attic and crawling around in the creepy basement to certify Glover Mansion is now "Ghost Free."

The most traumatic area was a place we called the Torture Room. The energy emanating from that room in the bowels of the basement was so putrid, it was downright nauseating. As we took a step into the room, we were practically knocked backwards as though a physical force had pushed us. It didn't take long for us to realize that something baaaad had happened in there.

As an empath, Ronnie immediately felt a strong knot in her stomach and a sudden rush of anxiety. She did **not** want to go back into that room. Laura Lee got really creeped out and started shaking from her core. Taking some deep breaths, we steeled ourselves and stepped inside. It was small and dark; no windows to let in any air or light. Visions started coming of people being beaten and locked in the tiny room. Overwhelming fear and anxiety permeated the space... blood, screams, pain, torture.

It took a while to get a portal established. Many Angelic beings were called on to help clear the space. The most amazing thing is after the last soul was finally set free and the energy was cleared, every pipe in the entire mansion flushed at once! You could hear the loud gurgling reverberating throughout the entire basement.

Neila, who was standing right outside the Torture Room door, just looked at us in astonishment. In all the years she had been there, it **never** flushed like that! This was confirmation that our work on a spirit and energetic level was triggering transformation in the physical.

Immediately after, the energy in the entire basement felt "flushed" and clean. Neila herself experienced a tremendous relief. The mansion, for which she felt such a stewardship over, was finally free and clear of the negative oppressive energy that had been so pervasive. Knowing she had completed her contract with it, Neila could now sell her home in good conscience. Not long after this final clearing, she was able to release the mansion to new owners.

Good-bye Momma!

Qi Gong Master, Rodger Estes was trying to sell his mother's home. She had passed away years ago, and he finally felt he was able to part with it. Of course it needed some repairs and remodeling, however, lots of disturbances created major delays. Paint cans would suddenly tip over, and contractors would quit unexpectedly, leaving the job in midstream. He was getting very frustrated because the work just wasn't getting done. So, who ya gonna call?

We were in the process of doing a TV news interview and the reporter wanted to film a **live** ghostbusting, so we had them meet us at Momma's house at sundown. A columnist for the local newspaper decided to be adventurous and tag along.

Walking through the empty house, we felt the presence of Momma in one of the rooms. Rodger then informed us it used to be her bedroom. We also felt the presence of another older woman. It turned out to be Momma's sister,

Ida. Apparently, they had died around the same time and had become trapped together.

After saying our prayers and setting up our altars, a portal of Light was opened and we invited the Angels to escort these women "home." They went peacefully. Then an amazing thing happened. Momma's house was across the street from a park. Entities that had been trapped there for years and years saw the Light, and started moving toward it. We literally had more than a hundred souls lined up to make the journey "home." There were Native Americans, a teenager who had committed suicide, a little boy on a tricycle, to name a few. The park had acted as a negative energy vortex because of the slaughter of Indians that had taken place in years past. On occasion when people in the surrounding neighborhood made their transitions, if their vibration wasn't high enough, they got sucked in and trapped there.

We patiently held the portal open until the last soul was able to cross over, and then cleaned up any remaining negative residue. The whole area felt so much lighter. We knew our work was complete.

Now that the interference was gone, the rest of the renovating went smoothly. When it had been completed, Rodger went over and put up a for sale sign in his mother's yard. A few minutes after he returned home, he received a call from a couple that had been driving by. They were from California and bought the house for cash that afternoon. How's that for record time!

This was our very first ghostbusting experience as a team. We worked together very synergistically and realized our talents complemented each other in opposite but powerful ways.

Necessity is the Mother of Invention
(Our First Remote Ghostbusting)

One of the theories in quantum (meta) physics is, "Beyond third dimension, there is no time or space, there's just now." Understanding this concept allows us to work remotely from the comfort of our own homes. We understood this in theory, but were able to put it into practice when Keith, an eighteen-year-old man from San Francisco contacted us because several ghosts were harassing him in his townhouse. It became so disturbing he voluntarily committed himself to a mental hospital!

Keith was desperate, and we knew he needed our help, *now*! Not having the luxury of making arrangements to travel to California, we decided to put our quantum theory to the test. This is the account of our first "remote" ghostbusting.

A consultation was completed with Keith, and after psychically investigating how best to proceed, we set up an appointment to perform the ghostbusting over the phone.

We each have different ways to prepare ourselves when making contact with the Spiritual realm. Ronnie says prayers and invokes her Angelic helpers, and Laura Lee contacts her assistants from other dimensions and realities.

When we were both ready and "in tune" we scanned the situation with a process very similar to remote viewing. As we checked in on Keith's home, we found there were indeed several different ghosts that had invaded it. No wonder he was so distraught!

It didn't take long to discover which ghost was creating the most problems. He was a military officer from World War II. Keith is of Japanese descent and this spirit was very hostile to him. He kept yelling at Keith, ordering him around, and telling him to, "Get out!" He felt this was **his** quarters and not only was Keith an intruder, but he was not where he was supposed to be as well. All Japanese people were sent to internment camps during WWII, and this ghost was in charge of enforcement.

The fact that Keith was free to walk around and do as he pleased caused great turmoil and anxiety for the disembodied military officer. He was then constantly barking orders at this young man. Keith, a First Wave Indigo, is very sensitive, and having this authoritarian, aggressive male spirit continuously on his case, created the feeling of being a prisoner in his own home!

After evaluating the situation, we realized that this military officer was not a religious man of any kind, but more atheistic in his belief structure. We then wondered how the heck would we get him into the portal. We had no idea how to handle this predicament since neither of us had run into it before.

Laura Lee finally requested help from her spirit guides to see if they had any ideas to remedy this dilemma. When she heard their solution, she laughed and shook her head in amazement...their idea was brilliant!

Laura Lee's guides told her that we needed to open a portal and bring back one of the ghost's superior officers to relieve him of his post. Then issue him new orders, which included being escorted by military personnel to his life review.

Laura Lee told Ronnie of the plan and she too was amazed at the brilliance and logic of this strategy. We opened a portal and there before us was a top brass officer. He saluted the ghost and told him he was being relieved of his duties, then gave him papers with his new orders. He was acknowledged for his service, and escorted by two beings that were also in uniform to the "other side." The ghost felt confident that everything was in order and he had done a good job. It was a win-win situation for everyone.

There was another ghost haunting the house that had been killed in the area in the late 1840's. He was a miner who had been double crossed by his partner and murdered for his half of the gold.

Ronnie saw that he was hit in the head when his back was turned. Dying instantly from the blow, his soul popped out of his body from the shock. He was furious as he watched his partner steal his pouch of gold.

As Laura Lee tuned into him, she realized that he was not going anywhere until he got his money back. It was this obsession that was keeping him stuck. All he wanted was his half of the money that had been stolen, and he wasn't leaving until he got what was rightfully his.

Laura Lee once again asked for assistance from her guides and guardians. She was not prepared for what happened next. All of a sudden, she could sense a part of her shifting into a finely dressed mid eighteenth century woman, wearing a long dress with a hat, and long fancy gloves. She walked up to the miner and opened her drawstring purse. Proceeding to pull out a handful of money, she said, "Here, I am going to give you all of your money now. Count it and make sure it is all there."

The trapped soul of the miner looked at her, completely mystified. He couldn't believe someone would just give him that kind of money. And the fact that it was coming from a woman made him shake his head in bewilderment. However, not wanting to look a gift horse in the mouth, he took the money and started counting it. When finished, he looked up and said, "Yup, it's all here, this is all of it."

Whewwww, Laura Lee was relieved that he didn't get ticked off that there wasn't enough money, or maybe even take a gun out and shoot her for trying to swindle him! She thanked her guides for helping her out on this one, and breathed another sigh of relief. Laura Lee and Ronnie then escorted the miner to the tunnel. He walked through continuing to count his money, very content and satisfied that he finally got what he had been waiting for. Another win-win situation.

The next ghost we encountered in Keith's townhouse was an ancient Japanese ancestor. We were still very new at ghostbusting so at that time, we had no idea what to do to help him. Then the Angels presented Ronnie with the insight to have Keith's father come back from the "other side" and assist, especially since it was probably one of his relatives anyway. That did the trick and it helped release some negative karma Keith's father had incurred for the way he had treated his son.

Now that Keith's insufferable intruders were eliminated, everything was quiet for a couple of days. However, on the third day there was evidence that time loop residue had manifested. Laura Lee was then able to instruct Keith on how to clean it up. Assisting him one last time a few days later, she neutralized and rerouted a ley line that was creating an energy vortex for aggressive, hostile frequencies and entities.

Things were nice and calm for a while and then Keith called again. He felt there was another ghost in his bedroom. He was absolutely sure of it, even though we had cleared that room. He insisted that the ghost was giving off an obnoxious odor. Laura Lee went ahead and rechecked the room...no ghost. Then she had a brilliant flash of psychic intuition and told Keith to check under his bed for the source of the smell. Guess what? Under there was a plate of food he had forgotten about. It had started to rot, and was responsible for creating the foul stench!

Keith was then certified "Ghost Free."

Here is a testimonial and note of appreciation from Keith.

I want to thank the Ghostbuster Gals for their help.

My ordeal started 1/11/02 to 1/14/02. During those three days of Hell, I was tormented by several entities, and one really mean male entity. I lost three days of sleep and was consistently harassed by that entity. I found the Ghostbuster Gals on the Google search engine. Thank goodness I did. I contacted them and told them my problem. Despite the fact I was calling from another state, they were willing and able to help me out. They told me that the mean entity had a military background, and he was angry and confused. Nonetheless, they managed to get rid of him and all the other hostile entities.

Thank God for the GBG's. I can finally get a decent night of sleep. Their professional help has really made my life a lot easier.

Keith in San Francisco.

It was about a year after that ghost clearing, when from out of the blue we got this letter from Keith.

Dear Laura Lee and Ronnie,
Hi, it's me Keith.
I'm glad to report the ghosts have not returned, especially the mean one.
Thanks for ghostbusting my home!
Keith

The Perturbed Professor

One of Ronnie's clients, Chris, was a house sitter for a friend named Marvin who was plagued by a ghost infestation. Marvin, a university professor, lives in a beautiful, newer home, but was being inundated by visitations throughout the house... the attic...the basement... and even the yard.

For the most part, Marvin ignored his uninvited houseguests, until his sleep began to be disturbed. In the middle of the night, he would be awakened suddenly by someone tickling his feet. One night he could actually see an indentation on the bed, and it felt like it was bouncing up and down. He lived alone and had no pets, so there was no rational explanation for this experience. That was it! He had to do something about this ghastly ghost situation. So, who ya gonna call?

Just prior to this, an independent videographer named Frank, wanting to do a documentary on the Ghostbuster Gals, approached us. Frank was impressed with the fact that after we did our work, not only could a tangible difference be experienced, but the paranormal activities disappeared as well. The main purpose of his film was he hoped it would be picked up as a cable TV show.

Frank and his wife, Gina accompanied us on our ghostbusting expedition hoping to get some good footage for his project. Since the professor was busy teaching, Chris let us in.

As we were standing in the kitchen, we looked out through the slider into the back yard and knew that was where we needed to start. An old platform that looked like it belonged to a tree house caught Ronnie's attention. She could sense the presence of a young boy out there.

Camera rolling, we headed out. Ronnie remembers it this way:

We stood by the platform and surveyed the area. There was more than one little boy present. His story would have to wait, as Laura Lee and I felt mysteriously drawn toward the back of the property. Without saying anything to each other we began to zero in on the same place. We knew it was Native American energy we were perceiving. The house was on ten communal acres of woods and brush and there I was in open-toed sandals. Nevertheless, I pushed on, mesmerized by this energy I was feeling.

All of a sudden, I heard Chris shout, "Ronnie stop! Turn right!" In shock, I did as I was told without thinking. "Now turn right again!" Heart pounding, slightly confused, I looked back to see that right in my path, had I put my foot down, was the biggest, fattest snake I have ever come across. We all looked at it in amazement. Interestingly enough, Gina was a herpetologist. She told us not to be alarmed, the snake, one of the largest corn snakes she had seen, was harmless. This snake, however, had me in its crosshairs and was zeroing in on me and my naked toes.

Gina tried moving the snake away with a stick, but that snake had only one thing on its mind... me. She kept telling us how unusual it was for this type of snake to be so aggressive. She also said she had never seen a snake behave in this manner.

It was astounding how the snake was so focused on me and only me. No matter what direction I would turn, it would head right toward me. No matter how Gina tried to direct it away, it would turn and lock on me again. Then the light bulb finally went on and I got it. I tapped into the Native American energy I was so intent on exploring and discovered the ghost of a medicine man. Laura Lee tuned into him and his agenda at precisely the same time! He was none too happy about having his sacred land encroached upon.

When I realized that the medicine man was controlling the snake, it literally stopped its fixation on me immediately and moved off. We were then free to continue our investigation. We ascertained that this Shaman and his three apprentices sacrificed themselves in an intense ceremony using poisonous snakes to help them cross over. This was done so they would have the power on the other side to guard and protect their tribe from the white man. (Boy, that worked well.)

While I was busy observing the Native's story, Laura Lee was creeped out by another presence in the area just behind the ceremonial ground used for the sacrifice. She was sensing the ghost of a female rape victim. Bringing this to my attention, I took a few minutes to tune into the energy Laura Lee had detected. It was pretty nasty. This young woman had been murdered by a man who raped and tortured her first.

After this disturbing discovery, we turned back to the medicine man. The snake had been sent by him to scare us off the land. Sensing we had psychic abilities, and were white, he did not trust us. He didn't want us to interfere in the mission that had kept him and his cronies there for so many years. Deciding to help these Natives right away (so they would not impede the rest of our work), we opened a teepee portal and brought their Chief back. He informed them that it was time to come home, their job was over, and they needed to leave with him now. They went willingly.

After our little outdoor adventure, we turned our investigation to the inside of the house. We decided to start in the basement and work our way upstairs. There, we found a young man hiding in the corner by the basement window. Knowing we were there, with the ability to make him leave, left this ghost a little apprehensive. As an aspiring artist, he loved being in the basement because that's where Marvin did his painting. Watching Marvin create art brought great joy to him, and he would actually inspire some of Marvin's work. After promising him he would be able to return once he crossed, he settled down enough to inform us that his name was Michael.

Moving up to the main floor, we are amazed to find that there were **no ghosts**! (Yea!) After a sigh of relief, we were now ready to take on the top floor. Chris told us that she felt some very uncomfortable energy in the walk-in closet and never wanted to go into that area. Access to the attic was there and it was in the attic that the next story begins.

Tuning into the area, Laura Lee and I discovered a terrified young teenage girl and her father. There was also an arrogant Ass Soul. This ghost's name was something like, Baron Von Gelderflug. (Sometimes it's really hard to get an exact name as we are interpreting a vibration.) He was the ringmaster of a circus/side show, and a very tyrannical, autocratic jerk. The father had worked for him and greatly feared the man.

The Baron exuded so much power and control, that when he decided he wanted to exploit the young girl sexually, the father turned a blind eye. The poor young woman had no one to protect her and was trapped both in life and in death, as the Baron continued his domination of her in the afterlife as well. These souls had died together in an accident and were somehow magnetized into the attic.

Checking out the bedroom we found the troublemaker responsible for disturbing Marvin's sleep. It turned out to be a little old lady who was drawn to him because in her confused state, she thought he was her son. So, she would sometimes bounce on the bed, tickle his feet and touch his face to get his attention.

Marvin owned a fairly new home, yet it attracted so many ghosts and we wanted to know why. When we checked it out, we discovered the real culprit. There was some strange energetic frequency in the attic that operated like an antenna for wayward ghosts. Marvin's inner light and meditation practices were also a beacon for them.

Successful Adventures in Ghost Deportation

Now that all the disturbances were accounted for, it was time for the busting. I set up my altar in the bedroom, and Laura Lee went into the offensive closet directly under the attic access. Preparing ourselves with prayer and meditation, we both received more details on all the ghosts we had found.

When we came together to compare notes, we decided to do the outside ghosts remotely from the bedroom window. By now it was dark, and I did **not** want to go outside and risk confronting any more snakes with my naked toes. As we were determining strategies for what to do with each ghost, Frank, still filming, laughed and said we sounded like two engineers consulting with each other on how best to solve a complex problem. We both laughed because in a way it was true!

Focusing on the young boy by the tree house, I was picking up the energy of another trapped soul in the vicinity. It was also a young boy who was sitting on the platform. His energy was not as strong as the first lad we had originally found.

I decided to established telepathic communication with the first boy under the platform. This is what was revealed. His name was Kenny, and he and his friend Fred were fooling around on the platform. They were roughhousing, playing "King of the Hill," when Fred got angry and gave Kenny a hard shove. Tumbling off the platform, Kenny broke his neck in the fall, dying instantly. At the moment of death Kenny experienced shock, anger, and betrayal. Unable to see the tunnel because of his low vibrational emotions, he became trapped where he died. Fred was absolutely devastated. In his head he knew he didn't mean to kill Kenny, but he still carried an enormous amount of guilt.

Tuning into Fred, the rest of the story crystalized. Not long after Kenny died, the farm where Fred lived caught fire and burned to the ground. Fred, along with his parents and grandmother, perished in the blaze. (This fire was confirmed at a later date.) When Fred left his physical form, his overwhelming guilt kept him earthbound. So connected with the energy of the accident in the tree house, he was drawn there hoping to find Kenny. The sad part of this story is that even though both boys were stuck in the same place, they never saw each other. Inhabiting different frequencies made them invisible to one another.

As Laura Lee and I opened a portal for Kenny, we did not see anyone come for him. He stood at the entrance looking a bit confused and unsure of what was happening. Then, all of a sudden, a little black dog appeared, and Kenny dropped to his knees in delight as the dog licked his face. This dog had been his very best friend in the whole world. Being ignored by his parents most of the time, his home life was miserable, but little Scamp loved him unconditionally. With Scamp in the lead, Kenny followed him "home," happy as he could be.

As for Fred, he was in such a low vibration, he did not recognize the portal. He just sat on the platform dejected and depressed. I told Fred how loved he was and that it was time to go "home," but he wouldn't listen. His guilt weighed so very heavily on him. I then explained that the death of Kenny was an accident and that Kenny had already gone through the portal and was waiting for him.

That got Fred's attention enough for him to finally see the tunnel. There was a great deal of hesitation, doubt, and fear as he looked at the Light. But, he just wasn't going. He felt he didn't deserve to go after what he had done. Then a most remarkable thing happened. There in the portal stood Kenny with his hand held out to Fred. Scamp was still by his side. Kenny had come back to help his friend cross. With such relief, Fred embraced his pal and all three of them went "home" together.

Now we were ready to connect with the rape victim and release her from her own self-induced hell. Not realizing she had already died, she was continually in a state of shock and terror thinking the rapist was going to come back and torture her again. So, she would stay as still and quiet as possible, "barely breathing" in a ghostly kind of way. It was difficult for us to communicate with her at first because she was "playing dead" and would not acknowledge our presence. We opened a portal and after trying several ways to get her attention, we were able to gain her trust enough to "sneak" her into the portal without detection from her killer...(At least that is how she perceived it.) Although she was traumatized, she was thrilled to see the Angels. Still not realizing she was dead, their love and compassion permeated her soul. Taking her hand, the Angels gently escorted her to the other side.

Immediately after she was gone, Laura Lee and I found two other women ghosts that had been hookers. They were the victims of a serial killer. He had been apprehended the year before, leaving a string of brutally murdered prostitutes in his wake. The interesting thing about these women is even though they were prostitutes, and had died horrendously, they were in a high enough frequency to see the portal. Having no problem heading for the Light, they joined the Angels for their journey "home."

We found one other soul on a street corner near the property...a young girl. She was a teenager that had been joy riding with a group of friends. Sitting on the trunk of the car, it accelerated and she slid off, hitting her head on the road. There was alcohol involved in these very bad choices that cost this young girl her life.

I had read about this incident in the newspaper a few months before the ghostbusting, but had no idea that it happened in the area close to Marvin's home. Later out of curiosity I asked about it and someone verified that the accident did indeed occur there. This lost soul was still in a foggy and confused state. However, she was able to see the Light and made a beeline for it.

Now that the outside area was clear, we turned our attention to the ghosts inside. Opening a portal in the bedroom, the Angels came to escort the old woman and the young man in the basement. Just before Michael crossed, he promised to come back after he had gone to "guide school" to help inspire

Marvin's painting. (He actually came back in record time and Marvin could feel his new muse assisting and expanding his artistic abilities.)

Laura Lee went back into the closet to determine how to handle the threatening energy in the attic. Taking a deep breath, she tuned into the Ass Soul ringmaster. He was one of the most sinister, abusive ghosts she had encountered. There was something "unearthly" about him... it felt like he didn't belong here. He was so arrogant, he was even trying to coerce and intimidate her...(Fat chance!) Laura Lee quarantined him in a Kryahgenetics Egg, which made him furious! He was **not** used to having any one but **him** call the shots. He began swearing, yelling and threatening her, while trying to extricate himself from the Egg...but no such luck!

Laura Lee ignored his rantings and began communicating with the young woman who found it hard to believe that anyone would have the guts to stand up to this tyrant to help her. When Laura Lee showed her the portal that was opened in the master bedroom, she saw the Angels there waiting to escort her "home." This miserable and oppressed young girl finally saw the Light at the end of the tunnel and eagerly headed for it. Laura Lee then assisted the young girl's father in recognizing the portal. He also was amazed that someone stood up to the ringmaster, but moved more warily because he was ashamed that he had lacked the guts to stand up and protect his daughter.

After they were both safely through the tunnel, Laura Lee realized she would need some help with the Baron. He was a different breed for sure. She asked her allies from the Dragon and Gargoyle realms to take the Egg (with its contents) to its proper place. Once they had taken him away, it was easier to clean up the electromagnetic residue he had left in the attic. When that was done, a huge shift in energy took place, and the entire area felt peaceful and light. The attic and closet no longer felt ominous and threatening. Now it just felt like an attic and a closet.

Successful Adventures in Ghost Deportation

Hungry and exhausted, we took a final scan of the area and happily pronounced it "Ghost Free."

Here is a letter from Marvin sharing his experiences of his haunted house.

> *My wife, Beth Ann and I first saw the place in the summer of 1993. She had a premonition we would live there, while I was attracted to a concentrated energy that permeated the site. Construction was completed, and we moved into it in the fall.*
>
> *From the very beginning, the house felt unsettled. It creaked and groaned like an old house that had more than its share of tragedy. Since childhood, I had experienced "paranormal" events; dreams of headlines that soon appeared in the local paper, apparitions of beings and, yes, I did see dead people!*
>
> *Beth Ann's reaction to the house was hardly serene. She was extremely uncomfortable for reasons she couldn't quite identify. This may have prompted her decision to move her business to Los Angeles where she would live full-time. I commuted because I was still working at the university in Washington. The "paranormal events" increased in number and intensity. I glimpsed shimmering beings, often someone, or something awakened me, bouncing on the bed, touching my face or tickling my feet. My sleep was interrupted almost every night, and I developed sleep apnea.*
>
> *Since I was away much of the time, I employed a house sitter, Chris, who had a similar reaction to the house as Beth Ann. She had several encounters with unknown entities, saw ghostlike beings and often found herself "creeped out" just being in the house by herself. One ghost, the "Baron," tormented her unmercifully by touching her and playing with the thermostat.*
>
> *Chris had a reading with Ronnie and asked her and Laura Lee to "ghost bust" the house.*

During the ghostbusting, Ronnie and Laura Lee encountered two young boys near an old tree house in the back yard. One of them had accidentally fallen to his death, and the other felt responsible. A little while after the clearing, a neighbor saw an article in the local newspaper about the Ghostbuster Gals. The story included some details about the work they did at my house and contained a couple of quotes from me. He made it a point to come over and confirm the fact that a long-time resident of the area recalled the death of the child at the tree house.

I cannot say enough about the positive changes we experienced after the busting. Not only was it successful, but my sleep improved dramatically, and the house calmed down and finally became livable.

Thanks for the help,
Marvin

The following excerpts are from the newspaper article mentioned in Marvin's letter. It is so fitting the story came out on Halloween Sunday.

REAL GHOST- GETTERS
By Heather Lalley /Staff writer

Ghostbuster Gals say they've freed dozens of displaced spirits.

Beware all you costumed ghouls and goblins, witches and warlocks, as you make your door-to-door rounds tonight. You might just run into some acquaintances of Laura Lee Mistycah and Ronnie Rennae Foster.

"Ghosts are simply trapped souls that need help," Foster says. "They are not demons," adds Mistycah, whose long black hair fits her nickname of "Witchy Woman." "They are displaced spirits."

Marvin Smith, chairman of the Electronic Media, Theatre and Film Department at Eastern Washington University says several of those displaced spirits took up residence in his Spokane home.

One young man would watch while Smith painted. Another more pesky spirit, an old woman in a cotton dress, would tickle Smith's feet and bounce on his bed.

"I don't do drugs, by the way," Smith jokes. "I'm mentally stable." However, Smith is steadfast in his belief in the spirit world. "It's not a belief," he says. " I know...I could always see spirits. Everybody is sensitive to this if they are quiet and pay attention. It's really a matter of paying attention."

Three other ghosts hung out in the attic, but Smith himself rarely had encounters with them. The Professor didn't mind the spirits much, but a friend who helps take care of his house persuaded him to let her call in the Ghostbuster Gals.

Mistycah and Foster, who goes by the nickname "Angel Girl," discovered even more ghosts than Smith was aware of inside and outside his two-story home.

They say they encountered the ghosts of two young boys near a tree house outside, one of whom had been pushed by the other one, Foster says. The fall killed him, but the other boy felt so guilty, his soul became trapped there too.

But things got even scarier when the two women nearly stepped on a large snake in the back yard. "It freaked me out, bad," Foster says.

In talking with the spirits, The Ghostbusters learned that the snake was actually being controlled by a Native American Shaman who had sacrificed his life for his tribe.

Back inside the house, Mistycah and Foster set up altars filled with crystals, angel figurines, sage, and Native American paraphernalia on each floor of the home. They "constructed" telepathic portals through which the spirits could pass.

The whole process took about six hours. But, apparently it was a success. "The spirits that were in my house are gone," says Smith.

According to a Harris Poll released last year, slightly fewer than half of the people who just read Smith's ghost story believe it holds as much water as a leaky bucket. The other fifty one percent, though, do believe in ghosts the poll found.

Mistycah and Foster have become accustomed to people thinking their ghostbusting is a little loony. That is until they need to give the Ghostbuster Gals a call, Mistycah says. "Then we're not so crazy."

The Ghostbuster Gals say they never met a spirit they couldn't set free. "We always seem to intuit a way to help them across," Foster says.

It's a good thing because their services don't come cheap. "It takes a lot out of us," Foster offered.

The Spokane area is full of haunted places, the Gals say. Ghosts like to congregate around cemeteries and hospitals, and in basements, attics and near fuse boxes...all of the places likely to give even non-believers the willies now and then.

"The reason people are scared is 'cause there **is** something there," Foster says.

Think about that the next time you need to flip a fuse, or grab a box from the attic. Maybe you'll want to bring a friend. (Or call the Ghostbuster Gals.)

Dannion's Domain

A few years ago, Ronnie had an opportunity to spend a couple of days with Dannion Brinkley and his lovely wife Kathryn, at his two hundred year old home in Aiken, South Carolina. Dannion is the bestselling author of, *Saved by the Light, At Peace in the Light* and newly released *Secrets of the Light,* which Kathryn co-authored.

After **three** near-death experiences, Dannion has literally transformed the consciousness of individuals on a global scale and is one of the foremost authorities on Death and the Afterlife. Dannion is also the founder of The Twilight

Brigade/Compassion in Action, a hospice volunteer organization that Ronnie has been involved with since 1998.

Here is Ronnie's account of that amazing adventure.

It's 1:00 am, Kathryn had already gone to bed and Dannion and I were sitting in the front room chatting. Out of the blue, I heard what sounded like a dog's nails clicking on the wood floor in the hallway. Looking at Dannion quizzically I said, "I didn't know you had a dog here." Dannion looked at me and casually replied, "I don't. That's Buddy. He died a long time ago." I was stunned. In fact, I thought Dannion was just kidding with me, so I jumped up to have a look for myself...**No dog.** The sound of Buddy's nails was so real and clear, it was hard to believe there was not a *physical dog* in the hallway! After my initial shock, Dannion confirmed that not only did he have a ghost dog in the house, but his Uncle Willy and Aunt Avis were there too.

Kathryn had given me a heads up about how haunted the house truly was, but I didn't remember anything about a ghost dog. A litany of complaints was shared with me about Aunt Avis who among other things was always rattling doorknobs and windows, and Uncle Willy who liked playing practical jokes on Dannion. One annoying thing he would do is cut the back porch light on and off and drive Dannion crazy. At first Dannion admitted, he thought it was faulty wiring and had an electrician come to check it out. But the wires were just fine and those lights still kept flicking on and off. After hearing about all the ghostly goings-on I thought, "This is a job for Ghostbuster Gals!"

The next morning, I spent some time tuning into Dannion's haunted habitat, then called Laura Lee. With the two of us at the helm, we went about the business of clearing Dannion's home.

When the job was finished, Kathryn felt the house was so much lighter, Buddy was not heard from again, no more rattling doorknobs and windows, oh, and the light by the back porch...it's working just fine.

Successful Adventures in Ghost Deportation

This letter is from Kathryn, expressing her gratitude for a peaceful house.

The ghost-busting talents of Ronnie Rennae Foster are truly beyond amazing! She walked into our home, in Aiken, South Carolina, in the summer of 2003, and changed the climate of our personal environment forever. The first time my husband, Dannion, asked me to visit his family home (built in 1804) he included a warning that it was haunted. He said that a great uncle, an aunt and her little terrier named, Buddy still lived in the house in spite of the fact they had all died between 1950 and 1989.

After my initial visit to the "haunted house," I realized this crowded arrangement was not going to work well for us. Aunt Avis seemed offended by our presence, and to let us know how she felt, she'd constantly rattle the doorknob to our bedroom while we slept. Once this tactic worked to awaken us, she would start the washing machine (a raggedy relic from the '50s) and torture us with the sound of its squealing motor. Buddy's energy also remained unchanged in the face of his death, and from dawn to the wee hours of the morning, he entertained himself by scurrying noisily across the wooden floors. Not wanting to be left out of the ghostly games, Uncle Willie would make his rounds about twilight each evening, to turn on all the ceiling lights throughout the house and flip the porch light on and off.

Our dead, but still feisty houseguests were amusing but, nonetheless, distracting. Dannion and I often discussed what to do about them. However, our opinions were diametrically opposed. I wanted them to go to the Light. Dannion felt they were having fun, and should be left alone. After five years of persuasive arguments, I won!

Ronnie just happened to be visiting her mother in Florida at the same time we were vacationing in South Carolina. I invited her to come spend some time with us, because we enjoy her company and I was hoping that when she perceived what was going on with our "terrorist tenants," she would know how to go about evicting them.

The first evening Ronnie and Dannion were sitting up talking when Buddy, true to form, went trotting down the hall. Ronnie actually thought we had a dog in the house!

The next morning, Ronnie spent the first few hours at our home just absorbing the energies and tapping into the personal stories of each of our invisible roommates. In the afternoon, she was ready to roll up her sleeves and go to work. She called her ghostbusting partner Laura Lee to help in the eviction.

We gave Ronnie her privacy in order to get the job done. Dannion and I went to lunch together, and when we returned home, we were astonished! The moment we walked through the door, we could feel the difference. The energy was lighter, and the scent of freshness danced in the air. As we walked from room to room, neither of us could detect the presence of our spiritual family. Both Dannion and I were absolutely incredulous. It felt like a brand new house! The Ghostbuster Gals had restored our home sweet home from a habitat of hauntings into a sanctuary of serenity.

We have no idea how Ronnie and Laura Lee did what they did, but to this day, Dannion and I are most grateful to Ronnie's genuine psychic skill, as well as her enormous love and generosity.

Welcome to the Hotel California

"We are all just prisoners here, of our own device."

In May of 2002 we were invited to Pahrump, Nevada as guests on the TV show, **Out There**. When we arrived, Kate and Richard the hosts of the show, mentioned that they had a close friend named Kathy who worked at the extremely haunted Amargosa Hotel and Opera House. The hotel was located at Death Valley Junction, in the middle of nowhere on the California/Nevada border. It was plagued with a plethora of ghosts and Kate thought given our profession, that we might be interested in visiting the place. How could we say no to such an offer? At the time we thought it would be a sightseeing tour, just to get our opinion on what was going on out there. Boy, were we wrong!

After about a forty-five minute drive through the desert, we pulled up to the hotel as night was starting to fall. It reminded us of the Eagles song, "Hotel California" with the palm trees, the stucco buildings, and a very eerie feeling emanating from it.

Kathy was one of the managers at the Amargosa. As a sensitive, she felt the plight of the spirits that were trapped there and was able to communicate with some of them. Most were very unhappy and under the thumb of one major tyrannical ghost. Once they came to warn Kathy that "*he*" was coming, and she needed to get out of there. They caught ghostly Hell from him afterwards for warning her!

Promising to find someone to help these gloomy ghosts, three attempts were made, with three different psychics. Unfortunately, they were all unsuccessful. Since Kathy had given her word, she kept trying. During this time, she also attempted to do what she could to make these oppressed souls, happy. She would actually have her husband come and play his guitar and sing. They recorded these sessions, and at the end of one they heard a man with a southern drawl say, "Thanks y'all. Love y'all." Kathy seemed to have a stewardship over this "flock of ghosts."

We were met at the entrance of the hotel by Kathy, and her parents, Don and Mary. Kathy began to share stories of all the bizarre things that went on since she began working there. One night a customer came bolting out of his room screaming. When they calmed him down, he explained that he was putting his things away when a cat came in the room. He had been distracted, but instinctively reached his hand down to pet it. When he did...he felt only **half of a cat**!

Another man, who was a military officer, reported that the room he was in was "unearthly," as the walls seemed to melt and another dimension opened. He was flabbergasted, and wanted to know if he could bring one of his superior officers over to check it out.

Kathy also had many professional film crews come to do documentaries, and invariably the batteries on all their equipment would drain, causing their lights and cameras to go out.

After regaling us with several more stories, and sharing some of the hotel's history, Kathy took us on a short tour of the lobby and the reception area. As we walked around, the energy was a little unsettling. Then the real "fun" began as we proceeded into the back dormitory section. This part of the hotel had not been in use for years. It was very dark, and we cautiously made our way over the junk and rubble.

We wandered about feeling a heavy, depressed, creepy energy throughout the area. Staying close together seemed to provide a modicum of safety. As we continued our exploration, we walked into a far back room. Ronnie immediately heard someone very distinctly shout in her ear, **"Geeeettttt Ouuuuuut."** Just at that instant Kathy commented, "Someone is not very happy that we are here." Ronnie laughed and told the group what she had heard. Laura Lee's psychic antennas just happened to go down at the time, (coincidence?) so she missed out on all the excitement. Everyone else was spooked as the air became charged and oppressive.

As we were walking past a broken down communal shower, Ronnie suddenly stopped and held her stomach. She saw a flash of blood splattered on the walls and floor. She saw the glint of a knife and a body slumped in a heap on the ground. Shuttering, she tried to compose herself. She made a mental note to help the poor soul that had died there so violently.

We continued on our tour, listening to countless stories of people that had either seen or heard ghosts, or had been the unlucky recipients of "ghostly hostility."

The main reason for all the malevolent, unearthly events that were constantly happening at the Amargosa was the vile, arrogant, tyrannical ghost that was squatting there. He thoroughly enjoyed controlling the other ghosts, making their life, or rather their "afterlife" a living Hell! This disincarnated soul was a jerk when he was alive and continued to be a jerk after he died. He was the very same ghost that screamed at Ronnie to get out, and was extremely angry at the intrusion into his territory.

Now that the tour was over, everyone looked at us expectantly. Our opinion was simple, **this place is as haunted as it gets!** There was no doubt about it. Then came the question, "Can you help?" We looked at each other feeling a little overwhelmed. We were not quite prepared to do the major ghostbusting required for something this big. Remember, we thought we were just going for a little visit to a haunted hotel.

Knowing that there were so many spirits that were trapped and in despair we decided to do whatever we could to relieve their misery.

As we walked outside, deep in our own thoughts of preparation and strategy, Laura Lee kept getting the vibe to go across the road from the hotel to an open field. There was an old abandoned gas station nearby. When she got there, the full moon was illuminating the area and she knew this was where we needed to do our work. She called to the others to come and join her. Everyone walked over (except for Richard, who didn't want any part of this eerie escapade), and we immediately formed a circle.

With the full moon streaming down around us, we knew the energies were perfect for what we were about to do. As we started to tune in, we could sense that not only were there ghosts in the hotel, but there were also many, many ghosts stuck in the field where we stood. It was almost like a "Ghost Bazaar," with tents everywhere, and we wanted to know why!

Laura Lee went around the circle with the two Aulmauracite rocks she just happened to have in her purse. As we held out our hands, she rubbed the rocks together, putting sparkly dust on everyone. She did this so that all would be protected by the stone of truth, ensuring truth and justice would prevail during this most vital undertaking. When it was Kathy's turn, she later reported that it felt like someone was mashing the dust into her palms as it sprinkled down. Kathy knew it was a "power rock" and so she assumed that it felt like this to everyone, (which it did not).

Holding hands, we began taking deep breaths to center ourselves as Ronnie led us in a visualization to elevate the vibration of the group. As Ronnie was speaking, Laura Lee noticed there was a man lurking in the corner of the gas station. He was just standing there watching us. She assumed he was a friend of someone in the circle, but at the same time, there was something not quite right about him.

All of a sudden, he started walking aggressively toward our circle, talking in a loud disruptive voice. We were shocked that someone could not see we were obviously engaged in some sort of ceremony and be rude enough to interrupt our endeavor.

Kathy then took the hands of the two people on either side of her, and joined them as she withdrew from the circle. She whispered, "Whatever you do, don't stop the ceremony! I'll take care of him." Apparently she recognized him as Eduardo, a mechanic in a nearby town. Usually he was very shy, reserved, and hardly said a word when he came to visit, but today he was bold and assertive. As he continued to talk in a loud offensive voice asking what we were doing, Kathy grabbed his arm and directed him back to the hotel for a cup of coffee. Eduardo walked with her across the road.

When Kathy reached the entrance to the office where Richard was waiting, he looked at her quizzically and said, "What are you doing back here?" She replied, "Well, I was just bringing Eduardo over for a cup of coffee." Richard looked extremely puzzled and said, "You're bringing who to do what?" Kathy turned to her left to introduce them, and Eduardo had vanished! He was nowhere to be seen. According to Richard, he watched her walk to the office alone, never seeing anyone with her. If Richard hadn't been unnerved before, he certainly was now!

Meanwhile, back in the circle, we intuitively knew we were being "messed with." We also came to the conclusion this was just going to continue because the hostile, Ass Soul knew what we were about to do, and was not going to give up his turf without a fight.

So without thinking, Laura Lee instinctively put a "Quarantine Kryahgenetics Egg" around this intimidating, diabolic ghost, and said, "Night, night" to him. She then lowered her hand from the top of the Egg to the bottom, slowly anesthetizing him. This was the first time Laura Lee realized we could put a "Quarantine Egg" around something. It has since come in very handy when dealing with powerful, enigmatic entities.

This dastardly "demon" was now in stasis, totally quarantined so he couldn't escape or interfere anymore. As Laura Lee was sedating him, he was ranting and raving and cussing, then all of a sudden, a horrible stench manifested.

It had the odor of rotten eggs, or sulfur or something equally disgusting, and we **all** smelled it. The stink was quite revolting, and it hung around for several minutes. Finally, when he was fully sedated, the obnoxious odor dissipated. His quarantined slumber gave us the freedom we needed to find out what was going on at the Ghost Bazaar and help the other trapped spirits out of the hotel.

As we tuned into this "city of tents" we could see that most of the ghosts looked sickly. There were men, women, children, plus some animal spirits as well. Judging by their clothes and our empathic connection, we determined it was about 1918-1919.

These ghosts all seemed to have died within a few months of each other. The pictures Ronnie was seeing were quite disturbing. She observed symptoms like extremely high fevers, with copious amounts of vomiting and diarrhea throughout the group. Whatever they had was obviously contagious because this area was a quarantined zone. Later we realized that around this time period there was a worldwide influenza epidemic that was responsible for killing millions.

We had just started to open a portal to free these suffering souls, when for some inexplicable reason, Kate started to fidget and exclaimed, "I don't know what's going on, but my guides just told me I need to go find Kathy." At that moment Ronnie also felt the impulse to leave the circle and sensed that she and the other two women needed to go back into the hotel to release the ghosts trapped there.

Ronnie and Kate walked back across the street and joined Kathy at the hotel. Then Ronnie and the two women, brave souls that they were, made their way in the near dark, to an inside hallway. There was no electricity available, but fortunately the moon shone dimly through some of the windows of the rooms with opened doors.

This was an area of great paranormal activity. In fact, not too long ago, as Kathy was carrying an armful of towels down the hall, she felt a push from behind and fell to her knees. The momentum and force was so great that she actually got carpet burns. This was the handy work of the big bad ghost we had just anesthetized.

The atmosphere was thick and stifling, as all the windows were closed. It was also hot, the air stagnant, and it felt deader than the ghosts. The lyrics to the song, *Hotel California* kept running around in Ronnie's head. "You can check out any time you like, but you can never leave." *"Well, we'll see about that,"* she thought.

As Laura Lee stabilized the portal in the field, Ronnie intuitively had the impression that another portal was needed right there in the hall. Interestingly enough, instead of having a direct portal to the "other side," she had the Angels connect her portal to Laura Lee's, resembling a bridge. It appeared as though there was some sort of energetic incongruity that was preventing the ghosts from leaving that area, and this bridge was the ticket to get them through.

At the exact moment the connection was made, Ronnie, Kathy and Kate suddenly felt a whooshing energy, as they physically experienced air rush by them. Their arms and faces could feel the breeze as the ghosts proceeded through the bridge. These poor souls that had been trapped in the hotel for so many years wasted no time in making their great escape. They could sense the tyrant wasn't around to keep them sucked into his realm. Kathy called out to them saying that this was the chance they had been waiting for and they needed to hurry. There was only one young man who was hesitant to leave. He was looking for his wife and couldn't find her. Ronnie assured him that he would eventually meet up with her and coaxed him into the bridge.

This was the first time Ronnie had physically and tangibly experienced ghosts. The hairs stood up on the back of all the women's necks, as each one perceived the same sensation. It was quite incredible!

Sensing that their job was done, the three ladies made their way outside to join the rest of the group.

Meanwhile, back at the circle, Laura Lee was holding the shimmering portal open with her arms. (She hadn't figured out yet that she didn't need to literally hold it open with her arms outstretched, and that she could use her mind instead, which was so much easier.) At a certain point she felt chills and a rush of energy.

Checking her watch, Laura Lee then saw and felt dozens and dozens of ghosts come from across the street into her portal. She then perceived one of the ghosts from the tent city. It was a young woman, waiting at the portal opening. She faced the hotel, expectantly. Laura Lee thought this was strange, but she just watched.

Then a young male ghost appeared from the bridge, and he embraced the woman in grateful relief. They entered the portal together, hand in hand. (We are pretty sure this was the ghost who was looking for his wife that Ronnie had persuaded into the bridge.)

When Ronnie, Kate and Kathy, returned to the field, Laura Lee asked what happened at 10:15 (the exact time she had looked at her watch and felt all the activity). Ronnie said that was just about the time she opened the bridge to the portal. What a coincidence, eh?

Now that Laura Lee had reinforcements, we continued to keep the portal opened. We then invited the tent city ghosts to cross over. Many Angels and sentinels were present to assist us. It took about twenty minutes to escort everyone through the portal. (Some of them even came back out of the tunnel to say, "Thank you.") This warmed our hearts and rewarded our efforts.

It was amazing to us just how many ghosts were stuck there. (Later we found out there was an underground waterway beneath the field. This most likely had something to do with the electromagnetic energy that was keeping the ghosts trapped.)

Next, we needed to determine what to do with the despotic, dark dictator that Laura Lee had kept in the quarantine Egg while all the other ghosts were rescued. She slowly brought him out of his slumber, and once again we could smell the putrid rotten egg stench as he awoke and realized he was still quarantined.

Phew! This guy was really angry at being confined as he was used to being the only one calling the shots. Once again, we were accosted by his swearing, threats, and overall offensiveness. Ignoring this (and trying to ignore the smell), we persisted. When the seething spirit saw the Angels, especially Archangel Michael, he finally realized what was going on. This made him more furious and he was **not** going to the Light through this portal. No matter how big the Angels were, they could not convince him otherwise. He believed that since he was such a mean, cruel, nasty son of a gun, the only place he would be going is directly to Hell, so he was just going to park his spirit butt **right there!**

Well, a little frustrated, we had to dig deeper to figure out what to do. As Ronnie tuned into this ghastly ghost, she got to see what made him that way. She witnessed the terrible life he led as a young boy. Her compassion flowed as she watched the mother he loved with all his heart, die when he was only ten.

Then Ronnie perceived the horrendous abuse his drunken father had heaped upon him. She saw how he was savagely beaten with a belt and how he went hungry for most of his childhood. He was treated no better than a dog and abandoned most of his early teen years. This is what turned a young sweet boy into the controlling Ass Soul that he became in life and continued in death.

Ronnie then got the brilliant idea to have one of the Angels bring this mean-spirited spirit's mother back through the tunnel and into the Egg with him. When his mother appeared, not only did this calm him down tremendously, but we were also astounded by the transformation in his countenance. He became softer, and then to our disbelief, he began morphing into a child again! We were stunned, as we had never seen this before. This is also the first time we received an inkling of his childhood name, as his mother called him Leo. She held him in her arms and murmured softly about how much she loved him.

Leo's mother apologized for his hard life and his abusive father. She expressed her sadness that she passed away and was not there to protect him. This confession of love melted Leo's steely, cold heart. He trusted his mother and took her hand as the Kryahgenetics Egg's energy field opened. Walking out together, they entered the tunnel of Light. Whewwww, what a relief for everyone involved, especially Laura Lee and her aching arms.

After the portal was closed and sealed, the heavy oppressive energy was totally lifted. Then the most amazing thing happened. We all simultaneously smelled another essence. This time instead of a disgusting odor...we smelled the wonderful sweet fragrance of roses! Even the crystal and Aulmauracite rock Ronnie held in her hands exuded the perfume of roses. Now, remember, we are in the middle of the desert, and there were absolutely *no* roses anywhere!

Exhausted yet exhilarated, we headed back to Pahrump to get a good night's sleep before the show.

In retrospect, every time we remember the night we spent ghostbusting the Amargosa, we always perceive the circle we had formed in the field, as though it contained at least twenty people in it. It seemed huge. However, when we account for the people that were actually there, we could only come up with a total of six. To this day it still boggles our minds!

News Flash: Cameraman Kirk gets Creepizoids From Dream Home

We think it is fitting that our last success story in this chapter is the conclusion of our first story in chapter one.

In our last episode, Kirk abandoned his "dream" home and was recuperating at his mother's, traumatized from the creepizoids. Here is the reason why. He had quite a gaggle of ghosts, animal spirits, and sleaze in the potato pit, all creating an enigmatic environment.

Since most of the disturbances in the house centered around the upstairs, particularly the yellow bedroom, we decided to begin our ghostbusting there.

Who was this energy that constantly harassed Kirk and his girlfriend? As Ronnie tuned in to the female presence we found outside the bedroom door, here is the story she received telepathically.

In the early 1920's, Spokane was an up and coming city. William Arthur McManus, Jr. was about to marry his high school sweetheart, Gertrude. His father, William Sr., a well-to-do banker, had just foreclosed on a lovely two-story home. It had only been lived in a short time, and he purchased it for a "song." The house became his wedding present to his son.

Over the next few years, things went well for the young couple. William Jr. took a job in his father's bank, and Gertrude gave birth to a beautiful little girl, they named Amanda Jane. Gertrude became pregnant again when Amanda was three. She wanted very much to give her husband a boy to follow in his footsteps.

One afternoon as Gertrude was folding clothes in the bedroom, she heard Amanda playing on the landing at the top of the stairs. The wood floors had just been polished until they gleamed. She started to warn Amanda to be careful, when suddenly she heard a thud and a small cry. Amanda had slipped and fallen down the stairs. Gertrude knew instantly as she ran to the railing and peered over, that her precious daughter was dead...her little body twisted in an impossible heap.

Things were never the same in the house again. Falling into a deep depression, Gertrude walked around in a fog, barely acknowledging her husband. She knew he blamed her for what happened to Amanda, just as she blamed herself.

When Gertrude's labor pains started, she had mixed emotions. *How could she be trusted with a new baby? She was such a terrible mother.* Gertrude's labor was long and hard. The trauma of her daughter's death played through her mind over and over as she was birthing her son. There were complications, she lost a lot of blood, and she also lost her will to live. Wracked with guilt and pain, Gertrude died while giving birth to the little boy she so desperately wanted. William, overcome by his tremendous loss, took the baby and moved out of the house. He could not stand to be reminded of how much had been taken away from him.

Gertrude died in such a heavy vibration of pain, guilt and despair, her spirit became stuck in the house. When Kirk bought it and started to remodel, she became very agitated, after all it was *her* house. Confused because Kirk actually looked a little like her beloved William, Gertrude vacillated between anger that her house was being altered, and longing for the husband she had lost. She particularly did not like Kirk's girlfriend. She felt Mary Ann was an intruder and did whatever she could to irritate her. Gertrude spent most of her time at the top of the steps wistfully staring down, wishing she could bring her daughter Amanda back.

When we were ready to set Gertrude free of her earthly bonds, Mother Mary came through the portal holding

Successful Adventures in Ghost Deportation

Amanda's hand. With enormous joy, Gertrude ran to her little girl swooping her up into her arms. At that moment, Gertrude got clarity and asked us to tell Kirk she was sorry for frightening him. She said he was a good man, and he deserved good things. Her parting words were, "I was confused. I am sorry. He can be happy now." With that, she was escorted "home."

As we scanned the rest of the house and property, we found more ghosts. Laura Lee kept sensing the energy of a dog, on the main floor near the staircase. It seemed that a previous owner of the house had a little boy who threw his puppy over the banister, killing him on impact. The little boy was indifferent, but the mother and older sister were absolutely appalled. That energy of revulsion and horror remained with the little puppy in the foyer. We made a mental note to remember to release this puppy through the animal/pet portal when we cleared the neighborhood.

Sensing some disturbances in the attic, we tuned into the energy psychically to investigate. Laura Lee found two older male spirits hiding there. Ronnie also saw these men, but found it difficult to connect with them. It appeared that they both had some kind of brain damage, or were mentally challenged and were very confused. The odd thing was that neither one of them could see or feel the other one. They just hung out there in a befuddled stupor, not knowing where they were or what they were supposed to do. It was actually relatively easy to help them cross as all we had to do was show them the portal that was still opened from Gertrude, and tell them to go there. They had no problem following directions.

After this, Laura Lee scanned the outside of the house. There was a small underground root cellar attached to it that had extremely repulsive energy. We humorously called it, "the sleaze in the potato pit" because that is exactly what it felt like. There was black magick, alcohol, drugs, sex, human excrement, and all sorts of riff raff energies in and around the pit. At one time, it seemed to have been the neighborhood hangout to do sordid and illicit things. We also sensed a rape had occurred there. When Ronnie felt just a quick glimpse of this nauseating vibration, she knew this was a job for Laura Lee, "Queen of Weird Sh!t."

It took a while, but Laura Lee did her "Witchy Thing" and cleared all the sleaze out of the potato pit. Since this area was like a magnet for psychic debris and pollution, having it cleared made a huge difference in the yard and entire neighborhood! Ahhhhhhhh...what a breath of fresh air!

Kirk then asked if we would tune into his dog, Logan. He had disappeared several months prior to our ghostbusting. Kirk thought Logan had dug under the fence and run away. However, he wasn't sure what had actually happened, or if Logan was even still alive. Wanting to help bring Kirk closure, we checked into the situation and came up with the unfortunate conclusion that Logan was dead. Kirk didn't seemed too surprised and mentioned that occasionally when he was on his back porch, he would catch glimpses of what he thought was Logan out by the fence. But when he would look again, nothing was there.

We established communication with Logan and saw that he was hit by a car not long after his escape. His spirit immediately returned to his Master and hung out by the back fence. Logan could feel Kirk grieving his loss, and told us that running away was a "baaaaad idea."

It was time to open a portal for the neighborhood ghosts and a Rainbow Bridge for the animals that were trapped.

We made sure the little puppy in the foyer was among the animals rescued. When it was Logan's turn, he started up the portal, but then bounded back to tell Kirk he was sorry for putting him through all the heartache. He then said good-bye and ran back into the portal. Subsequently something quite amusing happened. We saw that someone was waiting at the other end to give him a dog biscuit! Then the portal closed.

Relating this incident to Kirk, he said that it sounded exactly like Logan's personality. There was no question in his mind that we had indeed contacted his beloved dog.

Kirk told us that right after the ghostbusting things had calmed down tremendously but then...

It's Not Over Yet!

A few days later, we received another call from Kirk. The house felt so much better and lighter, however, the bedroom door where Gertrude had died, kept opening, no matter how many times or how hard he closed it. We scanned the room again and it seemed fine. Yet, upon closer examination of the energy, we did find another ghost hiding deep in the recesses of the closet.

The Rest of the Story

About twelve years after Gertrude left this world, William III or Billy as his father fondly called him, became gravely ill and passed away. Billy had always felt responsible for his mother's death, even though that sentiment was never expressed by the family.

Billy's father had often driven him past the old house, telling him stories of the mother he never knew. Billy felt very guilty, and longed for his mother who died giving him life. When his soul left his body, he returned to the very room in which he was born... the last place he ever felt his mother's energy.

Billy hid in the closet for many, many years. In fact when we did the original ghostbusting, there was so much other activity going on, we missed that closet completely. The amazing thing is, Billy and his mother never had contact with each other except in the womb. However, for some reason, Billy felt comfortable in the closet, somehow sensing her energy in the vicinity. Once his mother's energy was removed, he became agitated, feeling cut off and abandoned. In his confused state, he would repeatedly open the door, hoping to experience the energy with which he was so familiar.

We opened the portal outside the closet for Billy and brought his whole family back, to escort him "home." His mother was holding his sister Amanda. His father stood by her side. When Gertrude saw the son she never knew in the physical, she gave Amanda to her husband to hold and ran to Billy and hugged him. They all embraced and together disappeared back through the portal, the last vestiges of their energy going with them.

When it was all said and done, Kirk finally had the home he always dreamed of. The ghosts were gone, and the energy was clear and clean. Feeling safe and secure, he was now able to enjoy his time there in peace and harmony.

~ ~ ~ ~ ~

As you can see from our successful adventures, our clients have experienced dramatic and conclusive results from our ghostbusting endeavors. We pride ourselves in helping to make people's lives more comfortable and less stressed by the things over which they think they have no control. By removing the incompatible electromagnetic forces from their physical surroundings, people are free to lead happier, healthier lives, unobstructed by unearthly energies.

In Conclusion

We hope you have enjoyed your journey through some of our bizarre tales and unearthly adventures. Our purpose is to shine a light on the misunderstood, misperceived world of ghosts, and help advance the awareness that there is no such thing as death. A practical guide was included to provide a way for you to take command of your life and comprehend more fully the realm of Spirit.

We believe it is not enough to try to cast a trapped spirit out of a house or out of a person. That entity will often wind up squatting at the neighbor's, waiting for an opportunity to return. Ghosts need to be shown the way "home" so they can go through their life review and continue on their evolutionary path. Only then is there a win-win situation for everyone involved, and the Earth is a better place for it.

As you now may understand, many ghosts are lost and confused and in desperate need of help. We have heard their cries and have acquired the abilities and tools needed to rescue them from their torment, thereby alleviating the misery they may be creating for those who still walk this Earth.

So, if you ever find yourself in a situation where the hairs on the back of your neck standup, you get the "creepy crawlies" or the "Hee-bee-gee-bee's" and there is just way too much W.S. going on...Who ya gonna call?

3-2-1- Contact

For information and pictures you are invited to visit our website:

www.ghostbustersgals.com
(Make sure your speakers are on for the full audio experience. We have some really cool, spooky music on our site.)

Ronnie Rennae Foster

angelgirl@ghostbustergals.com

www.thetwilightbrigade.com
www.paths2connectedness.com

Laura Lee Mistycah

witchywoman@ghostbustergals.com

www.mistychouse.com
www.firstwaveindigos.com

Mystic House Publishing
816 W. Francis #244
Spokane, WA 99205

Cover art and photo by Laura Bold:
www.LBlightimages.com

In Conclusion

Ghostbusting Questionnaire

If you are considering a consultation with us, these are some of the questions you'll need to answer when we speak.

1. Describe what kind of paranormal activity you are having.

2. Has anyone been physically hurt?

3. How long has this activity been occurring?

4. Where is this activity taking place i.e.; house, apartment, mobile home, barn, car?

5. Are there any other places you have noticed these activities?

6. Who beside yourself is affected by this?

7. Can your pets sense this activity?

8. How old is the place of the paranormal activity?

9. What is the neighborhood like?

10. Do you know the history of the place and of previous owners?

11. Can you actually perceive communication with the entity?

12. Do you have any feeling of fear or dread when the phenomenon takes place?

13. What have you done to try to remedy the situation?

Shove-In Questionnaire

1. Who is having these experiences and for how long?

2. Describe the personality before and after.

3. How old is the person that is affected?

4. Was this person in an accident or rendered unconscious in any way?

5. Are there specific incidents that trigger unusual behavior?

6. Are drugs or alcohol involved now? Before?

7. Do other people notice the changes?

8. Can your pets sense any changes?

9. Can you perceive when the Shove-In is in control?

10. What percentage of the time is the Shove-In in control?

11. Have you done anything to try to remedy the situation? If so, has it helped?

12. Has the Shove-In ever communicated with you?

13. What do you hope we will accomplish?

In Conclusion

What's it Gonna Cost?

We endeavor to keep our prices very reasonable. There are a myriad of things that go into ghostbusting as you have witnessed throughout this book.

* These are introductory rates, please check our website for updates.

Consultation Fee: $150.00 ~ The consultation is about forty-five minutes. During that time we can "tune into" your situation and decide whether it is something we can instruct you in handling yourself or if you will need us or some other professional to help you.

Ghostbusting Fee: $250.00 per hour ~ (Plus travel expenses, if onsite work is necessary.) We have been very successful with remote Ghostbusting. This includes both our combined expertise and any ghostbusting paraphernalia we may need. **We always work together.**

Our Personal Agreement

* We guarantee the same ghost will not return.

* We pledge to help you make sense out of the senseless.

* We will continue to provide assistance after the initial ghostbusting if needed, to make sure all residual energy is cleaned up, in most cases at no additional charge. We expect our clients to be pro-active and follow our instructions.

* We are not responsible for the return of negative energy or neighborhood ghosts squatting on the premises due to drugs, alcohol, or violence.

Who Are The Ghostbuster Gals...Really?

Ronnie Rennae Foster
(Angel Girl)

Ronnie has her B.A. in Psychology. Since 1998, she has been the President of the Spokane Chapter of ***The Twilight Brigade/Compassion In Action,*** a volunteer organization that serves the dying. Under the auspices of Dannion Brinkley, world-renowned author of *Saved by the Light,* she is also a National Trainer for that organization, teaching volunteers how to provide a loving presence at the bedside of those making their transition. Recently, Ronnie was awarded a pin for the five hundred hours she has volunteered in the hospice ward of the Spokane, VA Hospital.

The Metaphysical Research Society of Spokane elected Ronnie to serve as their President three times. She is also an editor, teacher, empath, intuitive counselor, medium, ordained minister, trained as an emergency medical technician and is of course a Ghostbuster.

Ronnie gets her inspiration and insight from the Angelic Realm. Utilizing telepathic communication with Angels and Archangels, she is able to bring through information to help people on their spiritual path. The purpose of her work is to foster self-empowerment so her clients may reach higher levels of consciousness and make better choices for the evolution of their souls and the planet as well. She also teaches workshops on how to develop the intuitive skills to communicate with guides and Angels.

Contacting and conversing with souls that have previously made their transition to a higher dimension is an ability that took Ronnie years of hard work and meditation to develop. By implementing this gift, she can facilitate healing and assist with the grieving process, as well as apply it in ghostbusting.

Living on seven acres in the woods of Washington State, Ronnie shares her little piece of Heaven on Earth with her husband Jack, two cats, two dogs and two horses. Her only son Josh, has recently joined the Air National Guard and is proudly serving our country.

Laura Lee Mistycah
(Witchy Woman)

Laura Lee is the author of the books, *Kryahgenetics, the Simple Secrets of Human Alchemy* (now sold out and waiting for re-release in E-book), and also *Living in an Indigo House, the Heartaches and Victories of First Wave Indigos,* which is one of the first books released about Indigo adults. She has been in the cutting edge Healing Arts for over twenty years and developed many techniques that have facilitated instant healing and pain relief. She previously taught cutting edge Healing Labs that entailed training in foot reflexology, muscle response testing (Kinesiology) Electromagnetic Debris Sweeping, Muscle Skeletal Balancing and Kryahgenetics Emotional Release. She has clients all over the world. Laura Lee is the steward of *"The Knights of Mistyc House,"* and teaches Knights Training courses.

Laura Lee is also a solitary practitioner in Wicca and has developed her own "magick" methods and tools to reverse spells, curses, black magick and voodoo. Laura Lee has expertise in clearing all types of psychic, organic and metallic implants...and has found that most people with severe emotional problems have implants as the cause of their ailments...and a pill just doesn't fix it!

As a psychic and intuitive, Laura Lee can sense energies and entities that are out of balance or out of place, and then know how and where to redirect them. Laura Lee has a passion for working in the realms of Spirit, the Unknown and the Supernatural, and working with these energies has become normal and second nature to her.

Along with her humorous spirit guides, Laura Lee is also supported and protected by kind, intelligent, powerful, and benevolent Dragons, Gargoyles, and beings from other unearthly realms. Laura Lee also solicits the assistance of *Aulmauracite, the magical, mystical stone of truth and justice* in her healing work and especially in ghostbusting and implant removal. She won't do a session without it!

Laura Lee has four Indigo children who are now adults and off on their own adventures. She lives out in the country, and is currently working on another book entitled, *The Anatomy of the Porn Vibration*, (what they **didn't** teach you in Sunday School). This book reveals how the silent financial backers and promoters use this seductive and addictive insanity, to suck its victims into a black hole of destruction, all for greed, money and power!

Final Expressions

Now that you have finished our book, we hope you appreciated our sense of humor in what, to some, can be a very scary subject. If you have reached this point and still have not laughed even once, we suggest you check your pulse, then go back and read it again...because we hate to tell you this, **but** you just didn't get it.

We put our hearts and souls on the line by writing this book, and even though at times we do not resonate with some of each other's beliefs, it is our practice not to judge, but to respect the opinions and emotions of others. It is our wish that you will do the same.

In parting, the Divine Spark within us honors the Divine Spark within you (Namasté).

Thank you for reading our book. We hope it has empowered you!

Wishing you blessings, joy and humor on your journey in this life and the next,

The Ghostbuster Gals